Palermo
Trapani
Agrigento
Ca

Messina
Enna
tanissetta
AVERNA
Catania
Siracusa
Ragusa

The Silver Spoon

Sicily

THE ORIGINAL FUSION CUISINE

Like the layers of a timballo, its characteristic baked pasta dish, the essence of modern Sicilian cuisine has evolved from layers upon layers of the history of this island. It was a strategic location when the Mediterranean was the centre of the world, and each new conquering nation – and there have been many – left its seeds to create the unique composite we have today: sun-drenched produce from the land, aromatic and flavourful dishes and an abundant sea, which together create a rich, robust and varied cuisine.

Previous page:
Sicily's sun-drenched climate, abundant seas and enviable strategic location have all contributed to its colourful history of invasion and occupation.

The early indigenous population (2000–1800 BC) probably evolved from Neolithic migrants from Africa and the Arab peninsula. Trade eventually developed between them and the lands to the east, and it is likely that there were already a great number of fruits, capers, wild herbs and, naturally, seafood. It is widely believed that olives were introduced from the Aegean around 1300 BC.

In 735 BC the Greeks arrived to colonize the rich and fertile island, naming it Trinacria, or 'three promontories'. Naxos (near Taormina) and Siracusa were the first settlements, followed by Enna. By 700 BC, Palermo and other western settlements were established by the Phoenicians. Over the next 300 years, the Greeks developed the island, until the Carthaginians started territorial wars that lasted 100 years. Much of the Greek legacy is still visible today, from the elegant temples to elements of the local dialect; its impact on the cuisine is mainly agricultural. Besides bringing olives, pomegranates, grapes and the use of honey, the Greeks helped the island thrive with their farming methods.

Opposite and following pages:
Sicily's past as an outpost of both the Greek and Roman empires has left the island with many architectural treasures, such as the Roman mosaics at Piazza Armerina (opposite) and the Doric temple at Segesta (following pages).

In the second century BC, the territory-hungry Romans arrived to take on the Carthaginians and Greeks, and eventually took control of the island. Their contribution was to introduce hard wheat and

barley to feed their ever-expanding population, a crop that thrived in hot, arid Sicily. The Roman Empire was a distant and distracted landlord, and Sicily was subject to political disorder, religious persecutions and slave uprisings. Various barbarians plagued it until the Byzantines added Sicily to their empire in AD 535, which they managed to maintain for over 125 years.

If the Greeks made their contribution in agriculture, the Arabs (Berbers and Spanish Muslims, often called Moors or Saracens), who arrived in the early 800s, should get credit for many important new ingredients that took root over their two centuries of dominion: aubergines (eggplants), citrus fruits, apricots, watermelons, many spices, rice, seeds, nuts, dates, saffron and sugar cane. They are also credited with the ritual of mattanza, the method of trapping tuna and the practice of irrigation for crops.

Even more significant, however, was the Arabs' influence on the preparation of foods such as stuffed vegetable dishes, rice preparations like the elaborate timbale tummala, and pasta (particularly couscous). Sugar, especially, had a great influence in the preparation of pastries, a tradition that by the 1500s had been embraced by convents and monasteries as a vocation and source of financial support. Besides cassata and marzipan fruits, another ancient favourite that reveals Arabic roots is giuggiulena (also known as cubbaita, after the Arabic *qubbayt*), a brittle toffee with toasted sesame seeds and almonds. And perhaps the most important legacy is sorbetto (sorbet), which comes from the Arabic word *sarbat*. Credit the Arabs, also, for the use of spectacular aromatics such as flowering jasmine, rose petals and bergamot in refreshing drinks and ices. While the main city of the Greeks was Siracusa, the Arabs built up Palermo, a major stopping point between the east and Spain. Today, the markets of Palermo still share much of the excitement, colour and aromas of an Arab or Berber souk.

The Arab occupation of the island is responsible for many of the ingredients that make Sicilian food unique among the regional Italian cuisines.

The street markets of Sicily's towns and cities are overflowing with the abundance of fresh fruit and vegetables that are grown on the island.

In the late eleventh century, the Normans, led by Roger of Altaville, overthrew the Saracens. The Normans, with their Norse origins, introduced salt cod, which although might seem redundant in a land rich of fish, is still much appreciated today. The Normans ruled Sicily throughout most of the Crusades. In 1130, Roger II became the first King of Italy, which later passed to the German king Frederick I, and then to the French Charles I with the support of Papal Rome. The following years were rife with religious tension, and following the Inquisition many of the remaining non-Christians in Sicily converted to Catholicism. As old habits are hard to break, old pagan celebrations were replaced with Catholic saints, especially fertility rites, which is one reason why so many saint days are associated with particular foods.

The governance of Sicily was tossed back and forth, and it is likely that in the late fifteenth century, under the rule of Spain, New World ingredients such as tomatoes, bell peppers, squash and chocolate were introduced. Finally, in 1734, the Bourbon king Charles III presided until the French Revolution. During his relatively peaceful reign, the French influence started to be strongly felt in the kitchen. The noble families imported chefs called *monzú* (from the French *monsieur*), and added refinement to the local cuisine in the form of pâtés, galantines, rice gattó (gâteaux), layered and moulded timballi, and pastry-crusted savoury cakes. In 1860, Garibaldi ended the Spanish domination, and in 1861 Italy became part of the united Italy.

This mosaic of cultures resulted in a unique cuisine, but it would not have been possible without the Mediterranean climate and terroir of the island. Within its 25,000 square kilometres (9,500 square miles) there are many microclimates, ranging from desert-like conditions that can favour the cultivated prickly pear cactus (*fichi d'india*), to the mushrooms, nuts and cheeses of the mountains, and peaking at 3,300 metres

Following pages:
Sicily's varied landscape comprises lush and fertile mountains and valleys, a coastline rich with sea life and arid, desert-like planes.

(11,000 feet) at the top of Europe's tallest active volcano, Mount Etna. The volcano itself has created a soil rich in minerals and the perfect conditions for agriculture. In the hilly inland areas, wheat has been cultivated since Roman times, and still constitutes one of the largest crops. Along the balmy southern coast, citrus trees grow along with hothouses that produce some of Italy's first spring vegetables. The three expanses of water surrounding Sicily – the Ionian Sea (between Greece and Italy), the Tyrrhenian Sea (between mainland Italy and Sardinia) and the Mediterranean (the larger sea stretching from Spain to the Middle East) – offer some of the richest fishing grounds in Italy. It is never very cold at Sicily's lower elevations, and when spring breaks out, the air is filled with the aromas of orange blossoms, jasmine and almond flowers. Foragers return with baskets of wild asparagus, fresh herbs and artichokes... and, if weather conditions are right, mushrooms.

There is another distinctive feature of the island's cuisine: the contrast between the sea and the interior. In the past, people did not move from one area to another with vehicles as we do today, so if they lived even a short distance from the sea, they were not likely to eat much seafood. Salted anchovies or sardines were used as seasonings, but the main cuisine inland consisted of foraged and garden produce along with protein from pork, chickens, rabbits and sometimes beef. However, with over 1,000 kilometres (620 miles) of coastline, the sea was and is an important resource. One quarter of Italy's fishing boats are from Sicily, providing the rest of the country with tuna, swordfish, sardines, octopus and anchovies.

Earthy volcanic tones and the golden sun are reflected in the local produce. Vegetables grown in Sicily have singularly good flavour, and for that reason the dishes are simple, with nothing to mask their taste and quality. History, climate and terroir notwithstanding, much of the simplicity of the cuisine has to do with

Fish has a major part to play in Sicilian cuisine and the seas surrounding the island are teeming with life.

economy. While the nobles were feasting on elaborate French-style dishes, the majority of the country people developed a tradition of eating what was local, seasonal and often foraged, such as the minnows called *fragagghia*, tiny fish that are washed onto the shore in stormy weather. This cuisine is called *cucina povera* (peasant cooking), and is still the basis of most of today's dishes, which often have several variations ranging from very rich to quite sparse. Historians call this cultural stratification, and a perfect example is *pasta con le sarde* (Pasta with Sardines) (page 80), which in its richest form is pasta tossed with fresh sautéed sardines, wild fennel, saffron, raisins and pine nuts, and garnished with toasted breadcrumbs. When fresh fish was not available, other versions would use salted sardines, and in its poorest version may not have fish at all, called *pasta con le sarde al mare*, indicating that the fish have been left at sea.

Traditional dishes reveal regional differences due to microclimates and the varying availability of ingredients. Fish is made into fish cakes mainly in the south, and rolls in the Messina area; while around Palermo sweet-and-sour flavourings are characteristic; a common feature of the minor islands, meanwhile, is the use of capers, mint and oregano. Many of the most famous Sicilian recipes began as traditional local dishes and gradually became popular throughout the island, although they are best enjoyed in their place of origin.

Today, the sun-baked cuisine of Sicily is known throughout the world. Since the 1800s, many products have been exported. Most popular are the salted capers, canned tomatoes and tuna, cured anchovies and olive oil. Grapes have always been a major export as well, as the growing conditions are superb. The harsh climate made winemaking difficult in the past because temperatures were too high during the fermentation and ageing process, but in modern times with more sophisticated equipment,

Fresh fish, such as these anchovies, are on sale in the markets of the island's coastal towns within hours of being caught.

the region is producing many notable wines, among which twenty have achieved DOC status. While the province of Trapani, with its expansive area of vineyards, is considered Sicily's wine region, there are contributions from all parts of the island. The indigenous grapes include Catarratto, Grillo and Nero d'Avola (page 253), Malvasia, Zibibbo, Inzolia and several others, which are also sometimes blended with some foreign varietals such as Alicante, Cabernet Sauvignon and Merlot.

In the following collection of recipes, Sicily's traditional dishes will transport you to a world of simple preparations, colourful ingredients and rich, complex flavours.

Opposite and following pages: Sicily's winemaking regions produce many notable wines; among the most famous are Marsala and Nero D'avola.

TP 2062

I

TRAPANI

The northwestern coast of Sicily embraces the plentiful province of Trapani. Seafood, capers, olive oil and wine are exceptional in this area, as well as many artisanal ingredients. The starting point is the city of Trapani with its historic salt flats (page 32), also the home of a unique dish that is usually not considered Italian: couscous (page 39), served with a rich fish broth and stunningly fresh fish.

Previous page:
Fishing is the main economy of Trapani and the region's fishermen are famous for the mattanza technique that they employ when catching tuna (see page 50).

Although initially a Phoenician port, the charming fishing village of Mazara del Vallo, south of Trapani, is laced with Arab influences, including a Kasbah-style city centre. It is still one of the island's most important seafood ports, with the largest fishing fleet in the Mediterranean. You will find tuna and swordfish, of course, but also lobster, squid, grouper, mullet and red and purple prawns (shrimp), sold right off the boats as they come in.

This abundance has inspired many simple preparations that rely on the flavour of the primary ingredients more than the method. Near the salt flats at Paceco is the village of Nubia, the source of red garlic, an intense bulb that is red on the outside and white inside. Local almonds are ground with garlic and olive oil to make a pesto with tomatoes and herbs, which is served with fresh fish or tossed with pasta. Another favourite is handmade *busiati*, a pasta served with a lobster sauce. In Marinella di Selinunte there is a traditional festival celebrating the famed *sardine azure*, or blue sardines, which are skewered on canes and grilled over hot coals. Tuna has a long history in the area (page 50), and is found prepared in a variety of ways, from sweet and sour sauces with onion, bell pepper and fresh vegetables, to simply skewered and grilled. A ragù is also made from tuna, tunnina a ragù, and another favourite is *tarantello ammuttunatu*, a slice of tuna filled with garlic and mint and simmered in tomato sauce. The egg sacs that are removed from the tuna when they are caught are dried to become a splendid condiment called *bottarga*, which is grated over pasta.

Though Trapani is famous for its seafood, its climate is also perfect for producing a plethora of fruit, pulses, vegetables and nuts, such as these fresh almonds.

Trapani is the most prolific of Sicily's wine-producing regions and many of the islands most famous wines are made in the area.

The province of Trapani is known as wine country, with one of the largest areas of vineyards in Italy. The grapes thrive in the harsh inland landscape, and the fruit has long been a major export, but now with more advanced winemaking equipment they are able to produce several wines: Marsala DOC, Alamo/ Bianco d'Alcamo DOC, Delia Nivolelli DOC, Erice DOC, Salaparuta DOC, Menfi DOC, Moscato and Moscato Passito di Pantelleria DOC.

The inland cuisine includes rabbit, sausages and lamb roasted or grilled (broiled), with wild fennel always a protagonist. The black bread (*pane nero*) of Castelvetrano is made with whole wheat and allowed to rise very slowly, then baked in wood-burning ovens. Not to be missed are the exceptional cheeses of the area, such as *vastedda della valle del Belice*, the only sheeps' milk cheese that is a *pasta filata* ('spun paste'), kneaded and stretched under hot water.

Trapani province also has its own little mountain, the 800-metre (2,600 foot)-high Monte Erice (also known as Monte San Giuliano in the past) and its medieval village, often shrouded in a mystical fog, overlooking Trapani with a cable car that connects the two areas. The village is an important sacred place, the ancient site of the temple of Venus (the Phoenician Astarte or Greek Aphrodite), and is also the home today of several scientific foundations. Erice is also famous for its pastry shops, especially those of Maria Grammatico, the protagonist of the biography *Bitter Almonds* by Mary Taylor Simeti.

Following pages:
Trapani was founded by the Elymian's, but subsequently came under Roman, Byzantine, Arab and Norman occupation. While under Norman rule it played a part as one of the most important ports in the Mediterranean during the Crusades.

Sweets are made from almonds (and pasta reale or marzipan, see page 89), ricotta, figs, citrus fruits and honey. Some popular local sweets are: *belli e brutti*, *mustaccioli* (hard, spiced biscuits or cookies), *lingua di suocera* (a wafer called mother-in-law's tongue) and *genovese* (short pastry, shaped like ravioli and filled with pastry cream).

SALT

The Salt Road runs from Trapani to Paceco and Marsala. Here, you will encounter a series of lagoons with glistening pools of water and hills of sea salt mounded under terracotta tiles. Production of salt in this area dates back to the Phoenicians, thanks to the high salinity of the water and the perfect conditions of full sun, the hot, dry scirocco wind, and very little rainfall. The evaporation process begins with seawater being drawn into various shallow beds and left to evaporate. Old wooden windmills of the seventeenth century dot the eerie landscape, used at one time to pump the water and to power the grinding mill. As the salty water concentrates, the colours range from light green to pink until the final product emerges, a greyish white salt that is then harvested twice a year, usually around mid-July and mid-August, and raked into conical piles, then covered with tiles for protection until ready to grind and export.

The importance of salt cannot be underestimated. In times without refrigeration, it was essential for preserving foods for individuals, and also in commerce. It was a source of government revenue up until the 1970s, when the salt tax was abolished.

If you visit the area, be sure to see the Ettore e Infersa salt flats, named after two men, Ettore and Infersa, who restored a mill that is over 500 years old. There is also a Salt Museum in Nubia, where you can see old photos and the machinery used in the setting of a 300-year-old salt house.

The iconic windmills that populate Sicily's salt road were once used to drain water from the salt pools. Though no longer in use, many of the windmills still stand watch over the pools, where salt is harvested in much the same way as it has been for centuries.

CAPERS

The scrubby caper plant grows spontaneously from rock walls and rugged landscapes throughout the Mediterranean. Not easy to cultivate, some producers have actually managed to domesticate the plants to fulfil a growing market for this tasty delicacy. The best areas in Sicily are the Aeolian islands and on the island of Pantelleria.

Capers are actually the bud of a delicate white-and-purple flower, and if picked before the bud opens, can be cured and used in salads, pasta sauces and as a condiment for fresh seafood. They are harvested by hand every seven or eight days and immediately placed in a large container with sea salt. The salt draws out the moisture, which creates a brine that begins the curing process. After a month in their brine, they are drained and packed in coarse sea salt, and are ready to use once they have been rinsed.

If the flower blooms, from the purple-tinged stamen comes a secondary product, the caper berry (*cucunci* in dialect), which would ultimately become the seedpod. If picked at the right time, this can also be brined and used as a condiment. Capers are usually not cooked, but added at the end of cooking. They are delicious puréed into a pesto to top a crostini, and don't miss the recipe for Prawns (Shrimp) with Capers (page 36).

Capers preserved in salt and caper berries in brine for sale at a well-stocked market stall in Trapani. Both capers and caper berries are a mainstay of Sicilian food and are often added as a garnish or condiment after cooking a dish.

GAMBERI E CAPPERI

Prawns (shrimp) with capers

The best capers are those from the islands of Pantelleria and Salina. Their intense flavour is due to the iron-rich volcanic soil there and to the almost complete lack of rainfall.

Preparation time: 20 minutes
Cooking time: 20 minutes
Serves 4

- 500 g/1 lb 2 oz uncooked peeled prawns (shrimp), deveined
- 3 tablespoons olive oil
- 150 ml/¼ pint (⅔ cup) dry white wine
- 1 tablespoon small capers preserved in salt, rinsed
- 2 firm ripe tomatoes, seeded and cut into thin strips
- pinch of chilli powder
- 1 sprig flat-leaf parsley, chopped
- juice of 1 lemon, strained
- salt

Rinse the prawns (shrimp) under cold running water and drain well. Heat the olive oil in a frying pan or skillet, add the prawns, season with salt and cook over medium-high heat, turning them over with a wooden spatula, for a few minutes. Drizzle with the wine and cook until the alcohol has evaporated. Add the capers, tomatoes and chilli powder, then taste and add more salt if necessary. Cook for about 2 minutes, then sprinkle with the parsley, mix well and remove from the heat. Serve hot handing the lemon juice separately.

COUSCOUS

While the eastern and southern parts of the island seem more influenced by Greek traditions, the Arab influence is strongly felt on the western side. One excellent example of this is the traditional dish *cuscusu alla trapanese*, seafood couscous (page 40), which has origins in North Africa. Coarsely ground semolina grains are stirred by hand and hydrated in a terracotta basin called a *mafaradda*, forming small pellets that are then tossed with olive oil, salt and pepper, and steamed in a *cuscussiera*, a double boiler in which the upper pot is perforated like a colander. The cooking time is roughly one and a half hours, during which time a delicious fish broth has been simmering, to be served on the side. Variations on flavours include bay leaves and herbs, toasted almonds and occasionally cinnamon or cloves. Be sure to visit the fishing village of San Vito lo Capo for the annual international couscous festival, held during the third week of September.

Nowhere is the Arabic influence in Sicily more obvious than in the regular use of couscous, which has become synonymous with Sicilian cuisine.

CUSCUSU ALLA TRAPANESE

Trapani-style couscous

Preparation time: 2¾ hours + 2½ hours resting
Cooking time 45 minutes
Serves 6–8

— 1 kg / 2¼ lb (6 cups) couscous
— 2–3 tablespoons olive oil

For the fish broth
— 6 black peppercorns
— 1 onion, peeled
— 2 bay leaves
— 2 sprigs parsley
— pinch of saffron threads
— 2 kg / 4½ lb mixed fish, such as scorpion fish, grouper, sea bream, conger eel, cleaned
— salt

For the sauce
— 1 onion, very thinly sliced
— 1 clove garlic, peeled
— 2 tablespoons olive oil
— 800 g/1¾ lb tomatoes, coarsely chopped
— 50 g / 2 oz (½ cup) blanched almonds
— 2 tablespoons chopped flat-leaf parsley
— 500 ml / 18 fl oz (generous 2 cups) fish stock
— salt

For the couscousier
— 5 peeled tomatoes, chopped
— 1 onion, chopped
— 3 bay leaves
— salt and pepper

First, make the fish broth. Pour 1.5 litres / 2½ pints (6¼ cups) water into a large pan, add the peppercorns, onion, bay leaves, parsley, saffron and salt, cover and cook for 15 minutes. Add the fish to the pan and simmer for 30 minutes, then remove the pan from the heat and set aside until needed.

Meanwhile, put the couscous in a large dish. Whisk together 1.7 litres / 3 pints (7½ cups) warm water, the olive oil and a pinch of salt, then sprinkle the mixture over the couscous by hand. Separate the grains with your fingertips, cover with a wet dish towel and let stand for about 30 minutes.

Make the sauce. Pour water into a frying pan or skillet to a depth of 4 cm / 2½ inches, add a pinch of salt and heat. Add the onion and garlic clove and cook until the liquid has evaporated, then add the olive oil and cook, stirring occasionally, for 5–8 minutes, until the onion is lightly browned. Add the tomatoes, almonds and parsley, season with salt and cook, occasionally mashing the tomatoes with a fork, for 15 minutes. Remove the pan from the heat and discard the garlic.

Lift out the fish from the broth and remove and discard the skin. Remove and reserve any bones and flake the flesh. Set aside. Strain the broth into the tomato sauce, stir in the fish stock and cook over medium heat until reduced and thickened. Remove from the heat and keep warm.

To garnish

- 200 ml / 7 fl oz (scant 1 cup) dry white wine
- 2 tablespoons olive oil, plus extra for deep-frying
- 6–8 swordfish slices
- 6–8 baby squid, cleaned
- plain (all-purpose) flour, for dusting
- 16 uncooked prawns (shrimp), shells intact
- 1 bunch of curly parsley
- 1 lemon, sliced
- pepper

Despite its alarming appearance, scorpion fish is prized for its firm white flesh. Monkfish makes a good alternative.

Put the tomatoes, onion and reserved fish bones into the lower pot of a couscousier and season with salt and pepper. Almost fill with water, bearing in mind that it must not splash the upper pot of the couscousier during cooking. Bring to a boil and cook for 10 minutes.

Cover the perforated base of the upper pot with a well wrung-out damp dish towel, letting the 4 corners overhang the side. Separate the grains of couscous with your fingertips. Put the bay leaves on the damp dish towel and add the couscous. Cover with the lid and tie the opposite corners of the dish towel over it. Put the upper pot of the couscousier in place and steam for 20 minutes. Remove the lid of the couscousier, add half the sauce and all the flaked fish. Close the pan again and continue cooking for another 10–15 minutes. Turn off the heat and let the couscousier stand in the warm for 1 hour. Keep the remaining sauce warm.

Meanwhile, prepare the garnish. Whisk together the wine, olive oil and a pinch of pepper in a large dish. Add the swordfish slices and let marinate for 1 hour.

Heat plenty of oil in a shallow pan. Dust the squid with flour. Add the prawns (shrimp) and squid to the hot oil and cook for 5–8 minutes, until the prawns have changed colour and the squid are golden. Remove with a slotted spoon and drain on paper towels.

Put the couscousier in the centre of a warm serving dish and arrange the squid, prawns, swordfish slices, curly parsley sprigs and slices of lemon around it. Discard the bay leaves and serve immediately.

Coop. Mediterranea Pesca
ESCE FRESCO

OLIVE OIL

Olives are grown throughout the island, but it is those from Trapani, Palermo and Agrigento that are most prized for producing olive oil.

The olive was probably introduced to Sicily by the Phoenicians some time between the fourth and eighth century BC. By the time of the Roman Empire, Sicily had more olive trees than anywhere in the Mediterranean. The Arabs also appreciated the many uses of the olive, but under their rule the citrus fruit took priority. It wasn't until the Middle Ages that olives returned to grace and olive oil again became a valuable commodity.

The main provinces for olive oil are Trapani, Palermo and Agrigento, and several have DOP designations. There are over 30 indigenous cultivars used today, but the main types found in 80 per cent of the cultivation are: Nocellara Belice in the Trapani valleys; Nocellara Etnea in Catania; Biancolilla in Agrigento province; Santagatese, Nocellara and Oglialora in Messina; Carolea in Enna and Caltanissetta; Tonda Iblea in Siracusa and Ragusa, and Moresca in Siracusa. The olives have a wide range of colours from nearly white to green and red, and finally black when mature. The colour of the olive depends on the variety and the maturity, but in general, the riper (blacker) the olive, the more golden in colour the oil will be; the less mature the olive, the greener the oil will be.

The best oils are made with hand-picked olives. In the past, the mills used granite stones to grind the olive into a fragrant paste that would be stacked on mats and pressed, leaving the solids on the mat and expressing the liquid. Today, modern methods employ a sealed system that avoids oxygenation for a much cleaner and fresher product. The key, however, is starting with very fresh olives. The oil is usually about 14–18 per cent of the olive by weight, and in order to be called extra-virgin, the acidity must be below 0.8 per cent. Unfiltered oils have the best flavour and best health benefits.

Following pages:
Sicily's Saracen olive trees, so named because it is believed that some date back to the time of Arabic rule, are distinctive because of their huge gnarled trunks.

CERNIA AL FORNO

Baked grouper

Preparation time: 1 hour + 30 minutes standing
Cooking time: 1 hour
Serves 6

- 1 × 2-kg/4½-lb grouper, fins trimmed and cleaned
- 200 g/7 oz (1¾ cups) black olives, pitted
- ½ bunch of flat-leaf parsley, chopped
- 2 tablespoons chopped rosemary
- 1 tablespoon chopped oregano
- 10–12 cloves garlic, halved
- 200 g/7 oz firm ripe tomatoes, chopped
- 15 sprigs rosemary
- 50 g/2 oz (4 tablespoons) butter, sliced
- 200–300 ml/7–10 fl oz (scant 1–1¼ cups) olive oil
- 100 ml/3½ fl oz (scant ½ cup) dry white wine
- 2 lemons, sliced
- salt and pepper

For the dressing

- juice of 2 lemons, strained
- 100 ml/3½ fl oz (scant ½ cup) dry white wine
- olive oil, for drizzling

Sprinkle the fish with salt and let stand for 30 minutes. Meanwhile, slice 100 g/3½ oz (scant 1 cup) of the olives into rounds. Mix together the sliced olives, parsley, half the rosemary, the oregano, garlic and tomatoes in a bowl and season with pepper.

Preheat the oven to 230°C/450°F/Gas Mark 8.

Rinse the grouper and pat dry, then make several very deep diagonal slashes with a sharp knife on both sides of the fish. Season the inside of each cut with salt and pepper, stuff with the herb mixture and close each slit with a sprig of rosemary.

Sprinkle the bottom of an ovenproof dish with the remaining rosemary and a few slices of butter, drizzle 2–3 rings of olive oil and lay the grouper on top. Season lightly with salt and pepper, put the remaining olives and a few lemon slices in the cavity of the fish and secure the opening with a sprig of rosemary.

Cover the grouper with the remaining lemon slices and rosemary sprigs, spread any remaining herb mixture around the fish and drizzle with the wine and remaining oil. Bake for about 1 hour, until the flesh flakes easily.

Meanwhile, make the dressing. Whisk together the lemon juice, wine and a drizzle of olive oil in a bowl. Remove the fish from the oven, pour the dressing over it and serve.

TUNA

Fifty years ago the Sicilian coast was dotted with fishing villages and tuna processing plants. The shallow waters and currents provide the perfect environment for migrating bluefin tuna to reproduce, particularly at the island of Favignana. This is one of the last places you will see the famous mattanza re-enacted, more for tourism than actual commercial use. The mattanza, a rather brutal and bloody ritual was created by the Saracens for the harvest of these large animals. The event always took place in May, and began with the strategic placement of heavy nets weighted with anchors to create a passageway that channelled the fish into progressively smaller netted areas, until they reached the small and shallow 'death chamber,' where they were speared to the ritual chants called out by the head of the fishery. Once brought to the processing area on shore, they were gutted and cleaned, then cooked in ovens and preserved in olive oil.

Throughout the months of May and June the seas off of Sicily's coastline are teeming with bluefin tuna. The fish is widely used in Sicilian cuisine and forms the basis for many traditional recipes.

Today, the fishing industry employs the methods of spotter planes, long lines and drift nets year round, to great commercial success. A large percentage of the tuna goes to Japan for the sushi and sashimi market. To meet the demand, global tuna fishing has gone from under 500,000 tons to 3.7 million tons annually in the last fifty years. Scientists believe that the current worldwide overfishing practices are unsustainable, although many in the fishing industry will disagree. In an attempt to keep political calm, Japan exports their less desirable tuna to Sicily to replace the premium bluefin they import from the Mediterranean.

Fishing quotas are too high and attempts to create tuna farms have not been sustainable, and many of the egg-bearing females have been consumed indiscriminately, without allowing the population time to reproduce. Bluefin is nearing endangered status. If you visit the island, choose less rare species such as skipjack, yellowfin, albacore or bonito for your meal.

Following pages:
The port at Trapani remains an important base for the fishing industry as well as being a bustling transport hub.

GIUSEPPE C
TP 2200

TAGLIATA DI TONNO CON MIELE E PATATE

Preparation time: 30 minutes + 10 minutes marinating
Cooking time: 50 minutes
Serves 6

Tuna with potatoes and honey sauce

- 6 × 200-g / 7-oz tuna slices
- 3–4 myrtle leaves, shredded
- 1 clove garlic, thinly sliced
- 3 tablespoons olive oil, plus extra for drizzling
- 24 new potatoes
- salt and pepper

For the sauce

- 4 tomatoes, peeled and diced
- 1 tablespoon finely chopped flat-leaf parsley
- 1 tablespoon finely chopped chives
- 200 ml / 7 fl oz (scant 1 cup) red wine vinegar
- 4–5 tablespoons millefiori honey
- 2 tablespoons pine nuts, toasted

Preheat the oven to 200°C/400°F/Gas Mark 6. Put the tuna into a dish, season with salt and pepper, sprinkle with the myrtle leaves and garlic slices, drizzle lightly with olive oil and let marinate for 10 minutes. Heat 3 tablespoons of the oil in a frying pan or skillet, add the tuna slices and cook for about 2 minutes on each side. Transfer the tuna to a roasting pan and roast for 10 minutes, then remove from the oven and let stand for 10 minutes.

Make the sauce. Put the tomatoes into a dish and sprinkle with a little salt, a pinch of pepper the parsley and chives. Pour the vinegar into a pan, bring to a boil and cook until reduced by a quarter. Stir in the honey, remove from the heat and let cool. When the vinegar mixture is cold, stir it into the tomatoes, add the pine nuts and drizzle with oil. Taste and adjust the seasoning and let stand.

Blanch the potatoes in lightly salted boiling water for 10 minutes, then drain. Drizzle oil into a small frying pan or skillet and heat, then add the potatoes and cook over medium heat, turning occasionally, until golden and cooked through. Remove from the heat.

Put the slices of tuna on a serving dish and spoon the potatoes around them. Pour the sauce over the fish and potatoes and serve.

MARSALA

Marsala wine falls into the category of fortified wine, brought to international fame in 1773 by an English trader named John Woodhouse. Legend has it that Woodhouse landed in the port of Marsala and found the local wine very similar to the Spanish sherry that was already loved in England. In fact, the method of making Marsala wine was very similar to the solera method used in Spain, and Woodhouse began a commercial venture that he later sold to the Florio family, today one of the leading producers of Marsala.

The wine is made from indigenous grape varieties such as Catarratto, Grillo and Inzolia, and fortified with grape brandy at various points during the fermentation to yield three levels of sweetness: secco (dry), semisecco (semidry) and sweet. The colour can range from golden amber to ruby red, and the minimum ageing in wooden casks ranges from one to ten years or more.

The higher quality Superiore Riserva Marsala, Marsala Vergine and Marsala Stravecchio are served as dessert wine, and can also be paired with strong cheeses. Lesser quality and younger Marsala wines are frequently used in cooking, often served with meat, mushrooms and onions, such as Veal Escalopes (Scallops) with Marsala (page 58). Zabaglione dessert cream is also made with Marsala.

Giant oak casks storing Marsala wine at the Floria winery in Marsala.

125

SCALOPPINE DI VITELLO AL MARSALA

Veal escalopes (scallops) with marsala

Preparation time: 10 minutes
Cooking time: 30 minutes
Serves 4

- 500 g/1 lb 2 oz veal escalopes (scallops)
- plain (all-purpose) flour, for dusting
- 80 g/3 oz (6 tablespoons) butter
- 400 ml/14 fl oz (1⅔ cups) dry Marsala
- 2 tablespoons chopped flatleaf parsley, to serve
- salt

Dust the veal with flour, shaking off the excess. Melt the butter in a large pan and heat until it turns hazel in colour. Add the veal, in batches if necessary, and cook over high heat for 5 minutes on each side. Season to taste with salt, reduce the heat to low and cook for a few minutes more, then remove the veal from the pan and set aside on a plate in a warm place. Scrape up the sediment from the bottom of the pan with a wooden spoon, then pour in the Marsala, stir well and cook until reduced. Spoon the sauce over the veal, garnish with the parsley and serve.

BISCOTTI CON MARMELLATA DI CEDRO

Preparation time: 25 minutes + 30 minutes resting
Cooking time: 15 minutes
Makes 20

Biscuits (cookies) with citron jam

- 400 g / 14 oz (3¼ cups) plain (all-purpose) flour, plus extra for dusting
- 3 eggs
- 80 g / 3 oz (½ cup) caster (superfine) sugar
- 120 g / 4 oz (1 stick) butter, softened, or 100 g / 3½ oz (½ cup) lard
- citron jam, for spreading
- icing (confectioners') sugar, for dusting
- salt

Sift the flour onto the work counter and make a well in the centre. Break 2 eggs into the well, add the sugar and butter or lard and mix to an even dough. Cover and let rest in a cool place for at least 30 minutes.

Preheat the oven to 190°C/375°F/Gas Mark 5. Line 1–2 baking sheets with parchment paper.

Divide the dough into 4 and roll out each piece into a rectangle on a lightly floured surface. Beat the remaining egg with a pinch of salt and brush it over each rectangle. Spread the surface of the rectangles with the jam and roll up. Cut each roll into 5 pieces and mark the ends with a cross.

Put the biscuits (cookies) on the prepared baking sheets and bake for 15 minutes. Remove from the oven and transfer to a wire rack to cool, then dust with icing (confectioners') sugar.

II

PALERMO

A quarter of the Sicilian population lives in the province of Palermo, along the northwest coast. The capital city is also called Palermo, and the rest of the province includes townships such as Monreale, Cefalù and Bagheria. It is also home to the Parco Naturale delle Madonie, the natural park of the Madonie Mountains, which contains some of Sicily's highest peaks. The park is the source of many wonderful food products, a great number of them protected by the Slow Food organization, such as a cheese called *provola delle Madonie*, a unique bean called the *fasola badda* (badda bean) and manna, a natural sweetener that is extracted from ash trees.

The diversity of the sea and the mountains, and the culture of a unique city, Palermo, contribute to a synthesis of produce and history, of sweet and savoury, of noble and peasant. The skyline of Palermo is outlined with memories of the Saracen presence. Even though the conquering Normans converted the churches, many of the Arab domes and arches remain. As well as architecture, the table of today is still very much influenced by its early inhabitants.

The streets and the markets of Palermo are coloured with the abundance of the countryside, a bright palette of violet aubergines (eggplants), sun-brushed *arance tarocco* (blood oranges) from Catania, aromatic lemons from Bagheria, and the serpentine green cucuzza squash; giant swordfish with their swords held high, ugly yet delicious scorpion fish, mysterious sea urchins and sardines; spices, herbs and roasted onions; and tomatoes and garlic dangling next to bunches of explosively hot peppers. The clamour of the vendors harmonizes with the many smells. The markets bear witness to the cross-cultural food history and the many ingredients that are laced through the traditional dishes. The speciality of Palermo illustrates this: *pasta con le sarde* (Pasta with Sardines), bucatini tossed with fresh sautéed sardines, wild fennel, saffron, raisins and pine nuts, and garnished with toasted breadcrumbs.

Previous page:
The distinctive blue-tiled dome of the church of Santa Maria del Carmine in Palermo.

Palermo's lively streets are bustling with street-food vendors selling traditional favourites, such as arancini, panelle and, as shown here, crispelle.

ELLERIA DI CARLO
CRISPELLERIA

JAMES MORRISON
The Awakening
La Notte dell'Infiorata
XVIII Infiorata Artistica in onore del Corpus Domini
MARINEO
MARINEO
Giugno 2012
SVEN VÄTH
MAURIZIO SCHMITZ
CATANIA
SABATO 5 MAGGIO
LIBERA CULTURA
Presenta:

Palermo is known for its diverse culture and vibrant nightlife. The city is home to many venues that feature live music, ranging from traditional to modern.

Another favourite is *involtini di spatola* (Scabbard Fish Rolls), scabbard fish fillets rolled around a filling of pine nuts, breadcrumbs and currants.

Here, too, is the root of the Palermo street food tradition. Workers take a break, friends chat as they nibble on *panelle* (fritters made from chickpea flour, often served in a bun), *pane ca' meusa* (spleen sandwich), *arancini* (fried balls of rice stuffed with meat or cheese), *stigghiola* (grilled stuffed goat or lamb intestines), *crocché* (cheesy potato croquettes) and sfincione (focaccia topped with tomato and fried onion).

Holidays in Palermo, as in other parts of Italy, are associated with certain foods. In July, at the celebration of the patron saint of Palermo, Santa Rosalia, the celebratory dish is *babbaluci*, small snails seasoned with garlic and parsley and eaten with a cocktail stick or toothpick. At Christmas, the pan-Italian tradition of sharing panettone thrives here, too, but the local winter cake is *buccellato*, a round cake filled with almonds, pistachios, figs and other dried fruits. And what would Sicilian desserts be without citrus fruits, pistachios or sugar cane, imported by the Saracens? Today the world loves Sicilian cannoli and cassata. Both are based on fresh ricotta, preferably from sheep's milk. Ricotta is a secondary product in the cheesemaking process, 're-cooked' whey after the curd has been strained out. Cannoli are fried, tube-shaped shells filled with sweetened ricotta, candied fruit and/or chocolate. In the past they were served at Carnival (*Martedì Grasso,* or Mardi Gras), but today they are found in pastry shops all year round. Cassata, meanwhile, is an opulent dessert of liqueur-infused sponge cake layered with sweetened ricotta enhanced with pistachios and chocolate. The final touch is a layer of marzipan, and it is elaborately decorated with whole candied fruits. Once an Easter dish, it too can now be found all year round.

Following pages:
Palermo's diverse landscape comprises dramatic coastlines and craggy mountains, both of which contribute to the abundant range of produce that can be found in the area.

PULSES (LEGUMES)

In and around the small village of Polizzi Generosa in the Madonie Mountains, a small heirloom bean, called fasola badda in local dialect, can be found. *Badda* means 'ball', and these little bi-coloured beans are round like a tiny ball, with two colour variations, one ranging in colour from ivory with pink or orange markings, and another that is ivory with very dark purple stains. The badda bean has a distinct nutty, herbal flavour and is the protagonist in many soups and stews.

Two hours on a ferry north of Palermo rests the isolated volcanic island of Ustica, home to tiny lentils carefully harvested by a handful of families. A good source of protein, especially when combined with pasta, their miniscule size allows them to cook in a relatively short time (40–45 minutes). The traditional soup is made with vegetables and wild fennel, sometimes with the addition of broken spaghetti.

Ceci, or chickpeas, are a staple of most of the island. They are key players in soups and salads, and often appear as a side dish seasoned with olive oil and fresh herbs. Once dried, they can be ground to a flour used for the classic appetizer and street food, *panelle* (chickpea polenta), (see page 72). Broad (fava) beans have similar uses, but instead of grinding the dried beans for flour, they are flavoured with wild fennel in a soup or purée called *maccu*, a dish that goes back to the Roman domination. Another favourite dish is the *fritella* (or *fritedda*), a spring dish made of simmered wild artichokes, peas and fresh broad (fava) beans.

Chickpeas and garlic are hung up to dry. Chickpeas are a staple food in Sicily and are often used to bulk out salads or soups.

PANELLE

Chickpea polenta

It is traditional in Sicily to eat pane e panelle – a small bread roll filled with some very hot fried chickpea polenta sprinkled with lemon juice. The recipe is possibly of Arab origin – similar fritters can be found in Tunisia and other parts of the Mediterranean. In Italy, cecina from Viareggio and panissa from Liguria are similar.

Preparation time: 45 minutes + cooling
Cooking time: 15 minutes
Serves 6

- 250 g/9 oz (2¼ cups) chickpea flour
- 2 tablespoons chopped flat-leaf parsley
- olive oil, for brushing
- vegetable oil or lard, for deep-frying
- salt and pepper

Put the chickpea flour and a pinch of salt into a large pan and gradually stir in 600 ml/1 pint (2½ cups) water. Set the pan over medium heat and cook, stirring constantly, until the mixture comes away from the side of the pan.

Add more salt, if necessary, and stir in the parsley and a large pinch of pepper, then remove the pan from the heat. Brush the kitchen counter with oil, pour the mixture on top and smooth to a thickness of 1–2.5 cm/½-1 inch, then let cool.

Heat the vegetable oil or lard in a deep-fryer to 180°C/350°F or until a cube of bread browns in 30 seconds. Cut the chickpea polenta into rectangles, diamonds or squares, add to the hot oil, in batches, and cook until golden brown. Remove and drain on paper towels. Keep hot until all the batches are cooked, then serve with pre-dinner drinks.

INVOLTINI DI SPAGHETTINI

Spaghetti rolls

Preparation time: 1 hour 10 minutes
Cooking time: 30 minutes
Serves 6

- 7 tablespoons olive oil
- 18–20 large aubergine (eggplant) slices
- 700 g/1½ lb ripe tomatoes, coarsely chopped
- 3 sprigs basil
- pinch of chilli powder
- 400 g/14 oz spaghettini or tagliolini
- 4–5 tablespoons grated Parmesan or caciocavallo cheese
- salt and pepper

Heat 5 tablespoons of the oil in a large frying pan or skillet, add the aubergine (eggplant) slices in batches and cook over medium heat, turning once, for 12–15 minutes, until lightly browned. Remove with a fish slice (spatula) and drain on paper towels.

Meanwhile, press the tomatoes through a nylon sieve (strainer) into a shallow pan. Season with salt and pepper, add 1 basil sprig and chilli powder and cook over low heat, stirring occasionally, for 15 minutes. Remove from the heat, discard the basil sprig and stir in the remaining olive oil.

Preheat the oven to 180°C/350°F/Gas Mark 4.

Bring a large pan of salted water to a boil, add the pasta, bring back to a boil and cook for about 10 minutes, or according to package instructions, until al dente. Remove from the heat, drain and transfer to a bowl. Add 2 tablespoons of the cheese and about a quarter of the tomato sauce, shred the remaining basil into the bowl and toss well.

Spoon a little of the remaining tomato sauce over the bottom of an ovenproof dish. Spread out the aubergine slices on a board, put a little pasta on each slice and roll up. Put the rolls into the prepared dish, packing them tightly into a single layer. Spoon the remaining sauce over them and sprinkle with the cheese.

Bake for about 30 minutes, then remove from the oven and let stand for 5 minutes before serving.

COWS' MILK CHEESE

The distinctive shape of *caciocavello* cheese is achieved by tying the cheese by the neck and hanging them until mature.

Caciocavallo is a general term for cows' milk cheese made by stretching the curd in hot water. This method of working the curd is called *pasta filata* ('spun paste'), and gives the cheese a smooth, firm texture when aged. The name *caciocavallo* (*cacio* means 'cheese'; *cavallo* means 'horse', or can also mean astride) refers to the method of tying two cheeses by the neck and hanging them over a stick to mature, a little like saddlebags on a horse.

There are several types of caciocavallo in Palermo province, with variations according to the breed of cow and the local vegetation. One example is *caciocavallo Palermitano*, which is made in several villages, but mainly in Cinisi. The rich and aromatic milk is from a special breed of black cow called the Cinisara. The cheeses are usually around 3 kilograms (6¾ pounds), but can weigh up to 10 kilograms (22 pounds), are shaped into a square with a neck and are aged for up to six months. The result is a mild but nutty cheese.

Another treasure of this province is the *provola delle Madonie*, which is about 1 kilogram (2¼ pounds) and shaped like a pear with no neck. This fresh cheese has a delicate and sweet milk flavour, which you really taste because raw milk is used. It is delicious eaten as a table cheese with fruit or *salume* (cured meats).

The better cheeses are still produced in the traditional way: the milk is brought in twice a day and heated in a copper boiler, then coagulated with rennet. The curd is stirred with a wooden stick, the patella, to break it into smaller pieces and further release the whey. At this point, it can be gathered into muslin (cheesecloth) and shaped into a form to begin drying. After brining, the cheese is aged on wood shelves made of oak.

MALTAGLIATI CON L'AGGRASSATU

Maltagliati with aggrassatu

Preparation time: 15 minutes
Cooking time: 1 hour 20 minutes
Serves 4

— 400 g/14 oz maltagliati or pennette pasta
— 50 g/2 oz (½ cup) grated caciocavallo or Parmesan cheese

For the sauce
— 1 kg/2 ¼ lb veal silverside
— 25 g/1 oz (2 tablespoons) butter
— 2 tablespoons olive oil
— 4 onions, thinly sliced
— 1 clove
— 1 teaspoon cornflour (cornstarch)
— salt and pepper

Make the aggrassatu sauce. Tie the veal into a neat round with kitchen string. Melt the butter with the oil in a pan, add the onions and cook over low heat, stirring occasionally, for 5 minutes, until translucent. Add the veal, increase the heat to medium and cook, turning it several times and drizzling occasionally with water, for about 10 minutes, until evenly browned. Add the clove, season with salt and pepper, half cover the meat with water and simmer, stirring occasionally and adding more water if necessary, for 1 hour, until the sauce has thickened.

Remove the meat from the pan and reserve for a second course. Transfer the cooking juices into a small pan. Mix the cornflour (cornstarch) to a paste with 100 ml/3½ fl oz (scant ½ cup) water and stir it into the cooking juices. Set the pan over low heat and cook, stirring constantly, until reduced and thickened.

Bring a large pan of salted water to a boil, add the pasta, bring back to a boil and cook for about 10 minutes, or according to package instructions, until al dente. Remove from the heat, drain and transfer to a serving dish. Add the sauce and grated cheese, toss well and serve immediately.

PASTA CON LE SARDE

Pasta with sardines

Preparation time: 1 hour 10 minutes
Cooking time: 15 minutes
Serves 6–8

- 6 bunches wild fennel,
- 500 g/1 lb 2 oz sardines, scaled, cleaned and boned
- plain (all-purpose) flour, for dusting
- 150 ml/¼ pint (⅔ cup) olive oil, plus extra for drizzling
- 1 clove garlic, finely chopped
- 1 tablespoon chopped flat-leaf parsley, plus extra to garnish
- pinch of saffron threads, lightly crushed
- 1 onion, chopped
- 80 g/3 oz (½ cup) sultanas (golden raisins), soaked in warm water for 10 minutes, drained and squeezed out
- 80 g/3 oz (¾ cup) pine nuts
- 4 canned anchovy fillets, soaked in milk for 5 minutes, drained and chopped
- 500 g/1 lb 2 oz maccheroncini
- salt and pepper

Bring a large pan of salted water to a boil, add the wild fennel, bring back to a boil and simmer for 15 minutes. Remove with a slotted spoon and pat dry with paper towels, then chop finely. Reserve the cooking water.

Dust half the fish with flour, shaking off the excess. Heat half the oil in a large frying pan or skillet, add the floured sardines and cook, turning once, until evenly browned, then remove from the heat.

Heat 2 tablespoons of the oil with garlic and parsley in a shallow pan, add the remaining sardines, pour in 100 ml/3½ fl oz (scant ½ cup) water and simmer for 10–15 minutes. Mix the saffron with a little water in a bowl, then add to the pan, season with salt and pepper and stir to break up the sardines. Simmer for 10 minutes, then remove from the heat and set aside.

Put the onion, remaining oil and 100 ml/3½ fl oz (scant ½ cup) water in a shallow pan and cook for 5 minutes. Add the wild fennel, sultanas, pine nuts and anchovies and simmer for 10 minutes.

Meanwhile, bring the reserved cooking water to a boil, add the pasta, bring back to a boil and cook for 8–10 minutes, or according to instructions, until al dente. Drain, return to the pan and drizzle with olive oil, then stir in the saffron sauce and onion and fennel mixture.

Preheat the oven to 180°C/350°F/Gas Mark 4. Make alternate layers of pasta and fried sardines in an ovenproof dish, ending with a layer of pasta. Bake for 15 minutes, then remove from the oven, sprinkle with parsley and serve.

SFINCIONE

Sicilian pizza

Preparation time: 1 hour + 1 hour rising
Cooking time: 30 minutes
Serves 12–18

- 375g/13 oz (3¼ cups) plain (all-purpose) flour, plus extra for dusting
- 1 teaspoon salt
- 2¼ teaspoons fast-action (active dry) yeast
- 1 egg, lightly beaten
- olive oil, for greasing

For the topping

- 2 tablespoons extra-virgin olive oil, plus extra for drizzling
- 1 onion, thinly sliced
- 5–6 tomatoes, peeled and chopped
- 8 canned anchovy fillets, drained and chopped
- 50 g/2 oz pecorino cheese, sliced
- 150 g/5 oz mozzarella cheese, sliced
- 25 g/1 oz (⅓ cup) grated Parmesan cheese
- 50 g/2 oz (½ cup) pitted black olives, chopped
- 3 tablespoons capers, rinsed and chopped
- 2 tablespoons coarse breadcrumbs
- pinch of dried oregano
- pinch of dried chilli flakes

Sift together the flour, salt and yeast into a large bowl and make a well in the centre. Pour 250 ml/8 fl oz (1 cup) lukewarm water into the well stir with a wooden spoon, gradually incorporating the dry ingredients. Add the egg and stir to a soft dough. If the dough is too sticky, add a little more flour. Turn out onto a lightly floured surface and knead for 10 minutes, or until smooth and elastic. Shape the dough into a ball, place in a bowl lightly oiled with olive oil and cover with lightly oiled clingfilm (plastic wrap). Let rise in a warm place for about 1 hour, until almost doubled in size.

Preheat the oven to 220°C/425°F/Gas Mark 7. Brush a baking sheet with oil or line with parchment paper.

Make the topping. Heat 2 tablespoons of the olive oil in a frying pan or skillet, add the onion and cook over low heat, stirring occasionally, for 5 minutes, then remove from the heat.

Roll out the dough on a lightly floured surface, then transfer to the baking sheet. Spread out the tomatoes evenly on top and drizzle with oil. Bake for about 18 minutes. Remove the baking sheet from the oven and sprinkle the onion, anchovies, pecorino, mozzarella, Parmesan, olives, capers, breadcrumbs, oregano and chilli flakes over the tomatoes. Drizzle with oil if necessary and bake for another 10–15 minutes, until crisp and golden.

SCUMA FRITTA

Spaghettini fritters

Preparation time: 40 minutes + resting time
Cooking time: 50 minutes
Serves 4

- 300 g /11 oz very fine spaghettini
- 30 g/1 oz butter
- 150 g grated caciocavallo or Parmesan cheese
- 1–2 tablespoons aggrassatu sauce (see page 78)
- vegetable oil, for deep-frying
- salt and pepper

Boil the pasta in salted water until it is al dente, drain, dress with the butter and 2–3 tablespoons of parmesan, then stir in the aggrassatu sauce and season with freshly ground pepper.

Take a little mixture and roll it in your hand to form a small fritter. Place on a plate sprinkled with parmesan and continue until the mixture is used up. Sprinkle the fritters again with parmesan and keep under a weight for 30 minutes. Heat plenty of oil in a frying pan and fry the fritters until golden. Drain on kitchen paper and serve with the sauce of your choice.

CANNOLI

Cannoli

You will need about 20 metal cannoli tubes for shaping the dough. These are available from good kitchenware stores.

Preparation time: 30 minutes + 12 hours standing
Cooking time: 1 hour
Makes 20–22

- 150 g/5 oz (1¼ cups) plain (all-purpose) flour, plus extra for dusting
- 1 tablespoon lard
- 2 teaspoons white wine vinegar
- 3–4 tablespoons Malvasia wine
- 1 egg white, plus extra for brushing
- 1 teaspoon caster (superfine) sugar
- vegetable oil, for frying
- salt

For the filling

- 1 kg/2¼ lb (4½ cups) ricotta romana
- 400 g/14 oz (3¼ cups) icing (confectioners') sugar
- 50 g/2 oz (⅓ cup) candied pumpkin, diced
- 80 g/3 oz chocolate, chopped
- 2–3 tablespoons white rum

To decorate

- vanilla-flavoured icing (confectioners') sugar
- 4–5 shelled pistachio nuts, slivered

First, make the filling. Press the ricotta through a sieve (strainer) into a bowl, then add the icing (confectioners') sugar and beat with a wooden spoon. Add the candied pumpkin, chocolate and rum and mix well. Cover with clingfilm (plastic wrap) and refrigerate for 12 hours.

Make the dough. Sift the flour with a pinch of salt into a bowl. Add the lard, vinegar, wine, egg white and sugar and mix well to form a firm dough. Shape the dough into a ball, wrap in clingfilm and let stand for 30 minutes.

Cut the dough into 2–3 pieces and roll each out on a lightly floured surface. Cut out 20–22 squares or stamp out rounds with a fluted pastry cutter. Put a cannoli tube diagonally across each square, wrap the dough around it and seal by brushing with a very small amount of beaten egg white.

Three-quarters fill a frying pan or skillet with vegetable oil and heat. Add the cannoli, seam side down, a few rolls at a time, and cook, turning once, for a few minutes, until golden brown. Remove with a slotted spoon and drain on paper towels, then let stand until cool enough to handle. Remove the metal tubes and fill the cannoli with the ricotta filling just before serving.

Dust with icing (confectioners') sugar and decorate at the ends with the pistachio slivers.

MARZIPAN

Marzipan is a paste made of almond flour and sugar, which is used extensively to make the tiny, realistic fruit imitations called *frutta di martorana*, and provides the rich casing for the cassata. Known elsewhere in Sicily as *pasta reale* (named for Roger II, the Norman king of Sicily), in other parts of Italy it is called *pasta di mandorle*, or almond paste. The paste is made with whole blanched almonds (and the very occasional bitter almond), which are ground until powdery. Sugar is added, roughly 90 per cent by weight, although some commercial producers use equal parts. Colourings or flavourings, such as vanilla or almond extract, may be added. A small amount of water is added, and the paste is kneaded in a mixer until smooth and creamy.

The *frutta di martorana* are small fruit sweets moulded from *pasta reale* and hand-painted with vegetable dyes. They originate in a Benedictine convent in Palermo at the church of Santa Maria Ammiraglio (also known as the *chiesa della Martorana*). The convent, built in 1143 in the Piazza Bellini, was named for the Norman noble Aloysia Martorana. They were first created to decorate trees in the convent garden for the visit of an important church official, and were sold as a source of revenue until the 1900s. This tradition has carried on at many of the convents around the island.

The season for marzipan is traditionally in the autumn (fall), because that is when almonds are harvested. That may be the reason it was originally connected with Ognissanti, the feast of All Saints on the first day of November, and given to children as a present from their ancestors. By Easter, the season finishes with *pecorelle pasquali* (marzipan lambs).

Palermo is known for the dainty marzipan fruits that decorate the windows of confectioners' and pastry shops.

CASSATA SICILIANA

Sicilian Cassata

The Arabs brought this dessert to Sicily and the name 'cassata' is said to come from the Arabic *quas'at*, meaning bowl. The dessert was adapted in the sixteenth century by nuns, who were excellent pastry cooks, from the many convents on the island.

Preparation time: 1 hour + 24 hours chilling
Cooking time: 15 minutes
Serves 10–12

- 1 × 26-cm/10½-inch sponge cake

For the filling

- 120 g/4 oz (½ cup) glacé (candied) fruit, chopped
- 4 tablespoons white rum
- 1 kg/2¼ lb (4 cups) ricotta cheese
- 200 g/7 oz (1¾ cups) icing (confectioners') sugar
- 120 g/4 oz dark (bittersweet) chocolate, chopped

For the pistachio paste

- 50 g/2 oz (½ cup) shelled pistachio nuts, finely chopped
- 150 g/5 oz (1¼ cups) shelled almonds, finely chopped
- 50 g/2 oz (½ cup) icing (confectioners') sugar, plus extra for dusting
- 2 tablespoons white rum

First make the filling. Put the glacé (candied) fruit into a bowl, add the rum and let soak for 20 minutes. Meanwhile, beat the ricotta with the sugar in a bowl until smooth and even. Drain the glacé fruit and stir into the ricotta mixture with the chocolate. Cover the bowl with clingfilm (plastic wrap) and chill in the fridge for 12 hours.

Make the pistachio paste. Put the pistachios, almonds, sugar and rum into a blender and process to a paste.

Make the rum syrup. Pour 200 ml/7 fl oz (scant 1 cup) water into a shallow pan, add the sugar and heat gently, stirring constantly, until the sugar has completely dissolved. Bring to a boil and boil, without stirring, for a few minutes, then remove from the heat. Let cool slightly, then stir in the rum.

Rinse out a 26-cm/10½-inch cake pan with water and line with clingfilm (plastic wrap). Cut the sponge cake into slices and put half the slices side by side on the bottom of the prepared cake pan. Drizzle with half the rum syrup. Cover with the ricotta filling and top with the remaining sponge cake slices. Drizzle with the remaining syrup. Cover the pan with clingfilm and chill in the fridge for 12 hours.

For the rum syrup

- 50 g/2 oz (1/4 cup) caster (superfine) sugar
- 50 ml/2 fl oz (1/4 cup) white rum

For the decoration

- 2 tablespoons apricot jam or preserves
- 450 g/1 lb fondant icing (rolled fondant) or 200 g/7 oz (scant 1 cup) ricotta cheese creamed with 3 tablespoons icing (confectioners') sugar
- glacé (candied) fruit, to taste

Remove the cassata from the fridge, discard the clingfilm and turn out onto a serving plate. Heat the apricot jam with 1 tablespoon water, then brush it over the cassata. Either cover with the fondant prepared according to the package instructions or with the sweetened ricotta. Roll out the pistachio paste on a surface lightly dusted with icing (confectioners') sugar and stamp out diamond shapes with a cookie cutter. Brush them lightly with water and stick them around the outside of the dessert. Decorate the cassata with the glacé fruit and store in the fridge until ready to serve.

Cassata is a time-consuming dessert to make, most Sicilians would opt for the easier option of buying one from one of the island's well-stocked bakeries.

III

AGRIGENTO

The first impression as you arrive in the capital city of Agrigento is of the impressively intact structures in the Valley of the Temples, dating back to 400 or 500 BC. In February, fields of almond trees are profuse with white and pink flowers, and there are many recipes to reflect that. The province of Agrigento is wide and stretches from southwestern coast overlooking the temple of Selinunte to the southern exposure of Licata, and includes the Pelagie Islands that lie between Malta and Tunisia (Lampedusa, Linosa and Lampione). The cuisine is simple and fresh, and it relies on the many good products from the coast to the inland areas. The definition of the two zones becomes apparent within a short distance. People in the past didn't have the means of transportation that we do today, so seafood was mainly eaten by coastal inhabitants. Sardines and anchovies have long been preserved and traded inland, so there are many recipes that use them, but the inland cuisine was and is about delights like sausages marinated in wine; leg of Girgentana goat or mutton stuffed with breadcrumbs and cheese and roasted in a wood oven; and rabbit braised with wine and garlic, cooked with aromatic bay leaves and fresh vegetables. Preparations such as a marmalade made with cucuzza, a green squash, which is also used to make the *cucchiteddi* (cookies from Menfi) are also interesting. At the seaside in Sciacca, you find prawns (shrimp) with conza, a condiment made with toasted breadcrumbs, often called the poor man's cheese.

Previous page:
The Valley of the Temples in Agrigento is Sicily's most popular tourist destination.

Someone with a sense of humour came up with the name for *sarde a beccafico*. *Beccafico* is the small songbird that might come to mind when you see the sardine rolls with the tails sticking up like a bird's tail. The sardines are stuffed in the same way that hunters used to stuff the little birds, with breadcrumbs, pine nuts and raisins, and are delicious. Aubergines (eggplants) are prepared in an interesting way that harks back to harder times in a dish called *melanzane a quaglia* (quail-style aubergines/eggplants), because aubergines were substituted for quail. To simulate a bird, the round

The food of Agrigento focuses on good-quality ingredients, simply prepared. The markets of the region's towns are overflowing with wonderfully fresh produce.

Previous pages:
Agrigento's Valley of the Temples features many remarkably intact Grecian temples in the Doric style.

globe aubergines are sliced, deep-fried and served in a garlicky tomato sauce. Another evocatively named dish is pasta with carrettiera sauce, named for the local, colourfully painted wooden carts: a dish to satisfy a hungry driver, made with potatoes, olives and fresh, uncooked tomatoes.

Driving through the coastal hills, the cultivation of prickly pear (Opuntia) cactus becomes evident. It is prized for its magically coloured fruit called *fichi d'india*, or Indian figs. In the late summer, rows and rows of broad-leaf cactus produce succulent golden and magenta-coloured fruit that, once the spines are carefully removed, is delicious in sorbets and granite.

Besides the usual holiday preparations, you will find some unique dishes throughout the province of Agrigento. San Giuseppe contributes *pasta cu la muddica*, a spaghetti dish with sugar, cinnamon and chocolate. At Easter you might find *li cannilera*, made with cookie dough covering a hard-boiled egg and decorated with coloured sugar. The *taralli* (ring-shaped crackers) for the *Ognissanti* are sweetened with honey, sugar, chocolate, orange or vanilla.

Olives are grown throughout Sicily and are used both for eating and in the production of the island's famous olive oil.

PRICKLY PEARS

Previous pages:
The Girgentana goat, named after the region of Agrigento, is easily identifiable because of its distinctive spiralled horns.

Fichi d'india (Indian figs), as they are called in Sicily, are known as *nopales* in Spanish or prickly pears in English. The origins of the plant lie in the Americas some 500 years ago. This broad-leaf cactus plant is cultivated and thrives in the arid Sicilian climate and bears three colours of fruit: magenta/red, golden yellow and creamy white. The fruit has a spiny rind that can be removed by first slicing off both ends, then making a vertical slice down the length of the pear. Hold the pear with a fork inserted in one end and carefully peel back the skin from the lengthwise cut. The usual harvest is at the end of August, the *agostini*, but some producers remove the spring flower to force a second flowering for a fruit that ripens in the autumn (fall), the *bastardone*, which is usually much juicier, thanks to the seasonal rains. It can be eaten fresh, but is prized for making granitas, sorbets and other desserts.

Unique to Sicily, among the Italian cuisines, the prickly pear flourishes in the hot, dry climate. Its juicy fruits are mainly used in desserts.

ANCHOVIES

The ancient seaside town of Sciacca is known for some very good food, especially the salted anchovies. Fresh and cured anchovies find their way onto the tops of focaccia or bruschetta, or are rolled around almonds or sundried tomatoes. Fresh anchovies are often filleted and served simply marinated with lemon juice and olive oil. Cured, they are a key ingredient in many sauces, such as in Pasta with Anchovies (page 111) and the Anchovy Sauce that follows. The robust flavours of the anchovy have been used since ancient times, notably in garum, a liquid essence of anchovy juices and the salt used to preserve them, a by-product of the curing process. Today the methods have changed very little, and the product is called *colatura*; it is good on spaghetti, especially with *bottarga*. To serve or cook the preserved fish, remove them from the salt, rinse and soak in water for 15 minutes. Gently remove the spine to leave two small fillets and proceed with your recipe. If the opportunity presents itself, try fresh anchovies; they have a delicate, sweet flavour that belies the strong-smelling preserved products that have given anchovies a bad name.

Anchovies are abundant in the seas around Sicily and they are synonymous with the island's cuisine. Fisherman trawl for anchovies at night, luring them into their nets with light.

The first step is to bring in the little fish. From April to September, fishermen fish by night, attracting the fish into nets with a light. The best-quality anchovies have their heads removed immediately and are rinsed in brine to release much of the blood, resulting in a firmer and fresher fish to preserve. Once they have drained, they are salted to break down the cells and begin the preserving process. Sea salt from nearby Trapani is coarsely ground and layered with the fish under weights in large round cans for a couple of months. The liquid that is released during this process is the *colatura*. Alternative curing methods include brining the fish for two months, filleting it by hand and packing it in olive oil or vinegar. The oil-packed fillets are often ground into a paste that is packed in tubes: it should be used sparingly, as it is quite strong.

SALSA D'ACCIUGHE

Anchovy sauce

Preparation time: 25 minutes
Cooking time: 15 minutes
Serves 6

- 6 salted anchovies, cleaned
- 150 ml/¼ pint (⅔ cup) milk
- 3 tablespoons olive oil, plus extra for brushing
- 5 tablespoons breadcrumbs
- 4 tablespoons lightly crushed pine nuts
- 1½ teaspoons chopped oregano
- freshly cooked spaghetti, to serve

Open out the anchovies and put them on a board, skin side uppermost. Press along the backbones with your thumb, then turn the fish over and remove the backbones, snipping them at the tail end with scissors. Put the fish into a small bowl, pour the milk over them and let soak for 20 minutes to reduce the saltiness.

Meanwhile, brush a small frying pan or skillet with oil and set over low heat. Add the breadcrumbs and cook, stirring frequently, for 4–5 minutes, until crisp and golden. Remove from the pan and set aside.

Drain the anchovies, rinse under cold running water and pat dry. Heat the oil in a small, shallow pan, add the anchovies and cook over medium-low heat, stirring and mashing with a wooden spoon for about 10 minutes, until they have almost completely disintegrated. Add the pine nuts and oregano, stir rapidly and remove from the heat. Serve this sauce with freshly cooked spaghetti sprinkled with the crisp breadcrumbs.

PASTA CON I MASCOLINI

Pasta with anchovies

Preparation time: 1 hour 30 minutes
Cooking time: 15 minutes
Serves 6

- 6 bunches of wild fennel
- 500 g/1 lb 2 oz fresh anchovies, heads removed and cleaned
- 2 tablespoons chopped flat-leaf parsley
- 1 clove garlic, finely chopped
- 120 ml/4 fl oz (½ cup) olive oil, pus extra for drizzling
- plain (all-purpose) flour, for dusting
- 1 large onion, finely chopped
- 100 g/3½ oz (⅔ cup) raisins, soaked in warm water for 10 minutes, drained and squeezed out
- 100 g 3½ oz (scant 1 cup) pine nuts
- 4 salted anchovies
- 500 g/1 lb 2 oz maccheroncini
- 50 g/2 oz (1 cup) fresh breadcrumbs, toasted
- salt and pepper

Blanch the fennel in a large pan of salted boiling water for 1 minute, then remove with a slotted spoon and pat dry. Reserve the cooking water. Chop the fennel.

Put half the fresh anchovies into a shallow pan, add 2 tablespoons of the reserved cooking water, a pinch of salt, 1 tablespoon of the parsley and the garlic clove and drizzle with olive oil. Cook over low heat for 10 minutes, adding more cooking water if necessary.

Dust the remaining fresh anchovies with flour, shaking off the excess. Heat 5 tablespoons olive oil in a frying pan or skillet, add the floured fish and cook over medium heat until golden brown. Remove with a slotted spoon and drain on paper towels.

Pour water into a frying pan or skillet to the depth of about 1.5 cm/¾ inch, add 2 tablespoons of the remaining olive oil and a pinch of salt and heat gently. Add the onion and cook over low heat, stirring occasionally, for 15 minutes, until soft. Add the fennel, raisins, pine nuts, salted anchovies and poached anchovies and simmer for 10 minutes.

Meanwhile, preheat the oven to 180°C/350°F/Gas Mark 4.

Bring the remaining reserved cooking water to a boil, add the maccheroncini, bring back to a boil and cook until *al dente*. Drain the pasta, return it to the pan, add the remaining olive oil and the sauce and toss well. Make alternate layers of pasta, fried anchovies and breadcrumbs in an ovenproof dish. Bake for 15 minutes, then let stand for 5 minutes before serving.

GAMBERI CON LA 'CONZA'

Prawns (shrimp) with 'conza'

Preparation time: 15 minutes
Cooking time: 40 minutes
Serves 6

- 5 tablespoons olive oil
- 1 small onion, chopped
- 1 clove garlic, chopped
- 1 bunch of flat-leaf parsley, chopped
- ½ teaspoon chilli powder
- 500 g/1 lb 2 oz uncooked peeled prawns (shrimp), deveined
- 100 ml/3½ fl oz (scant ½ cup) dry white wine
- salt

For the conza

- 2 tablespoons olive oil
- 100 g/3½ oz (scant 1 cup) shelled almonds, chopped
- 100 g/3½ oz (2 cups) fresh breadcrumbs
- 1 heaped tablespoon grated Parmesan cheese
- pinch of chopped flat-leaf parsley
- salt

Heat the olive oil in a heavy pan, add the onion, garlic and parsley and cook over medium-high heat, stirring frequently, for a few minutes, then add the chilli powder and prawns (shrimp). Cook, stirring occasionally, for a few minutes. Drizzle in the wine and cook for 5 minutes, until completely evaporated. Remove from the heat and season to taste with salt.

To make the conza, heat the olive oil in a non-stick frying pan or skillet. Add all the conza ingredients, season with salt and cook over medium heat, stirring constantly with a wooden spoon to prevent the mixture from burning. It will be ready when it is golden brown. Serve immediately with the prawns.

SARDE A BECCAFICO

Sardines beccafico

Preparation time: 40 minutes
Cooking time: 30 minutes
Serves 4

- 800 g/1¾ lb sardines, scaled and cleaned
- red wine vinegar, for drizzling
- 1 large sprig parsley
- 2 cloves garlic, peeled
- 4 tablespoons grated pecorino cheese
- plain (all-purpose) flour, for dusting
- 2 eggs
- 100 g/3½ oz (2 cups) fresh breadcrumbs
- vegetable oil, for deep-frying
- salt and pepper

Cut off the fish heads, then open the fish up and put them on a board, cut side down. Press firmly along the backbone of each sardine with your fingers or thumb, then turn it over and remove the backbone, snipping it with scissors at the tail end. Rinse the fish, pat dry and put them, still opened out, in a large dish. Drizzle with a little vinegar and season with salt and pepper.

Meanwhile, chop the parsley with the garlic, then mix with the cheese in a bowl.

Put a little filling on one side of each sardine, fold the other side over and sandwich together, pressing down firmly. Spread out the flour in a shallow dish, lightly beat the eggs in another shallow dish and spread out the breadcrumbs in a third. Heat the vegetable oil in a deep-fryer to 180°C/350°F or until a cube of bread browns in 30 seconds. Coat the fish, first with the flour, then with the beaten eggs and, finally, in the breadcrumbs. Add to the hot oil, in batches if necessary, and cook for 6–7 minutes on each side. (You can also cook the fish in a preheated oven, 180°C/350°F/Gas Mark 4, for 30 minutes.) Serve hot or warm.

ORANGES

It is hard to imagine Sicilian cuisine without the ever-present citrus fruits at the table; their fragrant zest and juice are laced through most recipes, both savoury and sweet. Orange is *arancia* in Italian, a word that probably derives from the Arabic *naran*. Although the fruit has been settled in Sicily since the fourth century, the early varieties were sour oranges. The cultivation of sweet oranges began in the 1400s, and by the late 1800s they were a major export to northern Europe and beyond. It was around this time that a natural anomaly occurred and a new variety of orange was cultivated: the blood orange. Some people claim it may have been caused by the so-called Etna Effect, an unusual pigmentation caused by rapid changes in temperature caused by the volcano. However it came about, three varieties exist on today's market: the deep-coloured Moro, the sweet Tarocco and the Spanish Sanguigno, of which the Tarocco is the most popular, high in vitamin C and favoured for the orange, fennel and olive salad that often embellishes the winter table. Another delicious variation is sliced oranges with toasted almonds.

Citrus fruit is a common addition to Sicilian dishes and works beautifully with the oily fish, such as anchovies, which are another central component of the cuisine.

Citrus fruits grow well in Sicily's arid climate, and certain varieties have taken hold in specific geographic areas. Lemons and some mandarins are focused along the eastern coast and northern coast; the famous blood orange Tarocco, and its several clones, comes from near Catania; and in the area of Agrigento, navels, also called Brasiliane, are the main orange crop. Among the local varieties is the Ribera Vanilla Orange, a rare seedless orange with an aromatic vanilla perfume, which has DOP status (Protected Designation of Origin). A delicious table and juice orange, it is also used in various cakes, biscuits (cookies) and marmalades.

Following pages:
During the months that have cool nights and warm days, the trees in Sicily's orange groves are laden with juicy fruit. It is this variance in temperature that allows the Sicilian blood orange to thrive.

INSALATA DI ARANCE

Orange salad

The refreshing flavours of citrus fruit and fennel combined with the tasty piquancy of roast olives make this dish a perfect accompaniment to boiled or roasted meat. If you like, you can add to the ingredients.

Preparation time: 30 minutes
Serves 8

- 3–4 fennel bulbs, thinly sliced, fronds reserved
- 8 oranges
- 100 g/3½ oz (1 cup) roasted olives

For the dressing

- 5 tablespoons olive oil
- juice of ½ lemon, strained
- 2 tablespoons chopped flat-leaf parsley
- reserved fennel fronds (see above)
- 1 teaspoon fennel seeds (optional)
- salt and pepper

First make the dressing. Whisk together the olive oil, lemon juice, parsley, fennel fronds and fennel seeds, if using, in a bowl and season to taste with salt and pepper.

Cut off the peel from the oranges, removing all traces of bitter white pith. Cut the flesh into rounds, put them into a large salad bowl and add the fennel and olives. Drizzle the dressing over the salad, mix well and serve immediately.

ALMONDS

Almonds are abundant in Sicily and the flavour is found in many sweet and savoury dishes, from pesto to gelato.

Upon arriving at the Valley of the Temples in February, an evocative sight unfolds: the pink and white, delicate flowers of the almond trees against the backdrop of the ancient temples. Announcing spring, the first Sunday of February is the beginning of the week-long celebration of one of Sicily's major crops. Almonds (*Amygdalus communis L.*) have thrived in Sicily since the 3rd century BC; their origins are in central Asia, via Greece. Second in number only to olives, three categories of *Amygdalus* almonds have established themselves to become part of the Sicilian culture: the hard-shelled sweet *sativa*, the bitter *amara* and the soft-shelled *fragilis*. The bitter almonds, due to an element that converts to cyanide, are often used in non-food products such as cosmetics and oils. Rarely exported, the sweet almonds are used locally and extensively in classic Sicilian sweet and savoury dishes.

One famous product is the Arab-influenced almond-sugar paste, or marzipan, that is shaped into various fruits and vegetables and painted with vegetable dyes called *frutta di martorana* (page 89). Another favourite preparation is almond-infused water (known as almond milk), which makes a refreshing drink and an amazing gelato. Biscuits (cookies) such as amaretti also use sweet almonds. The almond biscuits called *'nzuddi* are the perfect amalgamation of two of the principal ingredients of the area: almonds and oranges. Created by nuns in one of the convents, the name *'nzuddi* is a nickname for Vincenzo, and were thus named for San Vincenzo.

NZUDDI

Almond biscuits (cookies)

The Italian name of these biscuits (cookies) comes from the diminutive form of Vincenzo – *vincinzuddu* or, in the Sicilian dialect, *nzuddu*. They were invented in Catania by the nuns of the Monastero di San Vincenzo.

Preparation time: 40–50 minutes
Cooking time: 10 minutes
Makes 30–35

- 200 g/7 oz (1¾ cups) plain (all-purpose) flour
- 1 teaspoon ground cinnamon
- 200 g/7 oz (1¾ cups) shelled almonds, roasted and chopped
- 200 g/7 oz (1 cup) caster (superfine) sugar
- 1 tablespoon finely grated orange zest
- 2 eggs
- 2 teaspoons baking powder
- juice of ½ lemon

To decorate

- caster (superfine) sugar, for sprinkling
- ground cinnamon, for sprinkling
- 100 g/3½ oz (scant 1 cup) shelled almonds, roasted

Preheat the oven to 180°C/350°F/Gas Mark 4. Line 1–2 baking sheets with parchment paper.

Sift the flour and cinnamon into a large bowl, add the chopped almonds, sugar and orange zest and mix well. Turn out the mixture onto a counter, make a well in the middle and break the eggs into it. Beat lightly with a fork, then add the baking powder and lemon juice. Continue to mix with a fork until the mixture is thick and slightly sticky.

Sprinkle the sugar and cinnamon for decorating in a flat-bottom bowl.

Take 1 teaspoon of the biscuit mixture at a time, roll into a small ball between the palms of your hands, then roll it in the sugar and cinnamon mixture. Put the balls on the prepared baking sheet(s) spaced well apart. Stick a whole roasted almond in each ball, pressing down lightly. Bake for about 10 minutes, until the biscuits (cookies) are light golden brown. Remove from the oven and transfer to a wire rack to cool before serving.

CCHI
PUNTO
SNAI
Lotto
BS 22
9925
PIAGGIO
HAWAÏ
BATH-ROOM
SURFER PARADISE
RALLYE DES PHARAONS

IV

CALTANISSETTA

Previous page:
The daily market in Caltanissetta features a vibrant mix of seasonal produce.

The province of Caltanissetta is shaped like an hourglass, and reaches from the Mediterranean Sea at the Gulf of Gela, an important oil refining port, to the centre of the island, where the capital city is located. The city of Caltanissetta, thanks to its central position, has long been a hub for commerce in the region. Its origins date back to the fourth century BC, and, like the rest of Sicily, Caltanissetta has been served by many masters. Sulphur mines were of great importance in the past, but today farming and wine are the main activities. Surrounded by agriculture, the daily market, *strata 'a foglia*, in the centre of town is vibrant with colours and aromas of the local and seasonal produce.

In the northern part of the Caltanissetta province, at the centre of the island, is the tiny village of Vallelunga Pratameno, home to the noble Tasca family since 1830. Their nearby 485-hectare (1,200-acre) estate, Regaleali, has earned international fame for their wines, and also for the cooking school and cookbooks of the late Contessa Anna Tasca Lanza. Nestled in the wheat and vine-covered hills, the property uses the sumptuous ingredients of the countryside, such as seasonal garden vegetables, fresh ricotta, pork sausages with fennel and estate-raised lamb.

Although there are some elaborate preparations in the restaurants of Gela and Caltanissetta, the local dishes are simple, *cucina povera* (peasant cooking) at its most elemental, though sometimes with a little flair. In Villalba, for example, cherry jam is added to savoury rice balls (*arancini*). *Cavateddi* is the pasta dish of choice, a fresh egg pasta with tomato sauce and seasonal peas or beans. Pasta served with a simple sauce of anchovies melted in olive oil, or polenta of semolina (*frascatula*) are other filling first courses, along with soups. The main courses include rabbit with olives and capers, and around Mazzarino you can enjoy *lumache a picchi-pacchi*, or boiled snails served in *picchi-pacchi*, a quick sauce of tomato, onion and garlic.

Like much of Sicily, the buildings of Caltanissetta are adorned with many architectural styles, reflecting the diverse range of occupation and influences that the island has fallen throughout its history.

Chicken is very popular, sometimes just simply grilled with a marinade of lemon juice and herbs. One of the more elaborate country dishes is the *pollo alla Nisenna*. A whole chicken is boiled in a vegetable-rich broth, then cut into pieces and rubbed with a paste of oil and fresh herbs, rolled in grated caciocavallo cheese and breadcrumbs, then roasted until crispy.

Many restaurants serve little pizzas called *fuate*, topped with fresh tomatoes, salted sardines or anchovies, grated pecorino cheese and fresh oregano. *Torta di giri sarbaggi* or *'mpanate* is also called focaccia, and is made with unleavened pastry dough wrapped around Swiss chard, ricotta and grated pecorino; another version in Niscemi is made with cauliflower and sausage.

Vegetables, wheat and pulses (legumes) abound. *Maccu* is a classic dish here, a purée of broad (fava) beans with wild fennel. Villalba is famous for its large green lentil, which is protected by Slow Food. At home, families enjoy a simple purée of *ceci* (chickpeas) garnished with a drizzle of olive oil. Niscemi has an annual artichoke celebration in the spring, featuring many different versions, such as stuffed or grilled. Near the coast, where citrus fruits flourish, a fresh salad of sliced oranges, onion and olive oil is enjoyed, and also a lemon version made with parsley, olive oil and bread.

Unique sweets in the area include *biscotti di San Martino*, which celebrate the saint in November, right after the religious celebrations of *Ognissanti e dei Morti* (All Saints and the Day of the Dead). It is a leavened bun sweetened and seasoned with anise seeds and cinnamon. Another sweet served for San Martino is *muffolette*, a roll of bread with fresh ricotta and local honey. You might also find blancmange flavoured with lemon zest, and the village of Delia is known for *cuddrireddra*, a sweet biscuit (cookie) with a long tradition (page 139). In Campofranco, *virciddrati* are made with a shortcrust pastry filled with dried figs, orange zest, cinnamon and candied mandarin.

Garlic is used sparingly in many Sicilian dishes. Its strong flavour provides a fragrant warmth to sauces and marinades, but it can be overpowering if used to excess.

LIQUEURS

Since the Italian meal starts with an *aperitivo* (apéritif) to stimulate appetite, it follows that *amari* (bitters) are an important finish; they are considered helpful for digestion. Every area has its own recipes, usually infusions of herbs, flowers or fruits in food-safe alcohol. Some are made with artichokes (Cynar), distilled beetroot (beet) molasses (Fernet) or rhubarb (Zucca), but the common elements are an alcohol content of 25–40 per cent and a pleasantly bitter taste. Some names you might recognize: Averna, Ramazzotti, China Martini and surely Campari. Caltanissetta native Salvatore Averna founded Averna in 1868. Averna was a supporter of the Benedictine Convent of Santo Spirito. As with many convents and monasteries, the monks created elixirs for health reasons, and to express their appreciation for his support, they passed their secret recipe to Salvatore Averna. The rest is history, as they say. The *amaro* found its way onto the table of the royal family in the 1900s, and Vittorio Emanuele III gave Averna the authority to print 'Exclusive to the Royal Family' on their label, quite an important stamp of approval. The product quickly gained widespread popularity and became known as a digestive drink.

Today, after four generations, the business remains in the family, and the recipe is still a secret. The description of the ingredients in the liqueur is a bit vague, but includes 'roots, herbs, citrus rinds and caramel colouring.' There are distinct spicy and woody aromas, while the flavour is fruity with tones of vanilla, cinnamon and liquorice.

The liqueur Amaro Averna is synonymous with Sicily. It is enjoyed at the close of a meal.

SPAGHETTI CON AGLIO, OLIO E PEPERONCINO

Spaghetti with garlic, oil and chilli

Preparation time: 15 minutes
Cooking time: 20 minutes
Serves 4

- — 5 tablespoons olive oil
- — 2 cloves garlic, thinly sliced
- — ½ chilli, chopped
- — 1 sprig flat-leaf parsley, chopped
- — 350 g/12 oz spaghetti
- — salt

Heat the oil in a small pan over low heat, add the garlic and chilli and cook, stirring occasionally, for a few minutes until the garlic is golden brown. Season lightly with salt, remove the pan from the heat and stir in the parsley.

Bring a large pan of salted water to a boil, add the spaghetti, bring back to a boil and cook for about 10 minutes, or according to package instructions, until al dente. Drain, tip into a serving dish, add the garlic mixture and toss well. Serve immediately.

PASTICCIO DI POLLO

Chicken pie

Preparation time: 1 hour 45 minutes
Cooking time: 45 minutes
Serves 6

- 300 g/11 oz (2⅓ cups) plain (all-purpose) flour, plus extra for dusting
- 70 g/2¾ oz (⅓ cup) sugar
- 100 g/3½ oz (7 tablespoons) butter, plus extra for greasing
- 50 g/2 oz (⅓ cup) lard
- 2 eggs
- 2 tablespoons Marsala

For the filling

- 3 tablespoons olive oil
- 1 × 1.2-kg/2½-lb chicken
- 500 ml/18 fl oz (generous 2 cups) hot chicken stock
- 50 g/2 oz (½ cup) shelled pistachio nuts, peeled
- 50 g/2 oz (½ cup) shelled almonds
- 100 g/3½ oz (2 cups) fresh breadcrumbs
- 2 eggs, lightly beaten
- 2–3 tablespoons chopped flat-leaf parsley
- 1–2 tablespoons drained capers, rinsed
- juice and grated zest of 1 lemon
- salt and pepper

First make the filling. Heat the olive oil in a shallow pan, add the chicken and cook over medium heat, turning occasionally, for 10 minutes, until lightly browned. Drizzle with 100 ml/3½ fl oz (scant ½ cup) of the stock. Simmer, adding more stock, a little at a time, for 40 minutes, until the chicken is tender. Remove the pan from the heat, let the chicken cool, then remove and discard the skin and cut the meat from the bones.

Dry-fry the pistachios and almonds in a small frying pan or skillet over low heat, shaking the pan frequently, for a few minutes until just golden. Remove from the heat and chop coarsely.

Pour the remaining stock into a bowl and soak the breadcrumbs, then drain. Mix together the breadcrumbs, eggs, parsley, capers, lemon juice and zest, chicken and chopped nuts in a bowl. Season to taste and stir gently.

Preheat the oven to 180°C/350°F/Gas Mark 4. Line a 24-cm/9½-inch round cake pan with greaseproof (wax) paper and grease with butter.

To make the dough, sift the flour into a bowl, add the sugar, butter, lard, 1 egg and the Marsala and mix well to a smooth dough. Divide the dough into 2 pieces, 1 larger than the other. Roll out each piece into a round. Put the larger pastry round in the bottom of the pan, spread the filling over it and cover with the second round. Lightly beat the remaining egg. Decorate the top of the pie with pastry trimmings and brush with the beaten egg. Bake for about 45 minutes, until golden brown. Remove from the oven and let stand for 5 minutes before serving.

ITALIAN BISCUITS (COOKIES)

The sheer variety of Sicilian biscuits (cookies) is mind-boggling, and alters from province to province, according to the local ingredients and traditions. Many are tied to holy days, but nowadays you can find most sweets all year round. Some of the traditional biscuits include *cuccidata* (fig and honey biscuits), *buccellato* (filled with dry fruits, nuts and chocolate), *nucatoli* (S-shaped filled biscuits), *reginelle* (sesame seed biscuits), *mustaccioli* (hard, spiced biscuits), *lingua di suocera* (a wafer known as mother-in-law's tongue) and the *genovesi* (short pastries shaped like a ravioli filled with pastry cream). In Caltanissetta province, the specialty is the *cuddrireddra* of Delia, ring-shaped to symbolize a crown, in tribute to the noble women of Delia who lived in the medieval fortress in the late thirteenth century. The dough is made with semolina flour, eggs, sugar, butter, red wine, cinnamon and orange zest. Strips of dough are spiralled around a wooden dowel, with two lengthwise strips sealing the shape on each side, then rolled on a textured surface to seal the shape. Once slipped off the dowel, the twirled strip is closed into a ring shape, then fried in olive oil. Originally, it was a typical sweet prepared during Carnival, but today it can be found all year round in the bakeries of the area.

The crown-shaped biscuits (cookies) *cuddrireddra* are unique to the town of Delia. They are traditionally enjoyed during Carnival.

BISCOTTI DEL CONVENTO

Preparation time: 35 minutes
Cooking time: 20 minutes
Serves 6

Convent biscuits (cookies)

- 500 g/1 lb 2 oz (4 cups) plain (all-purpose) flour
- 125 g/4¼ oz (scant ⅔ cup) caster (superfine) sugar
- 1 egg
- 1 egg yolk
- 100 g/3½ oz (7 tablespoons) butter or lard, softened
- 50 g/2 oz (⅓ cup) cream of tartar
- pinch of bicarbonate of soda (baking soda)
- grated zest of 1 lemon

To decorate

- 1 egg white
- few drops of lemon juice
- 100 g/3½ oz (scant 1 cup) icing (confectioners') sugar

Preheat the oven to 190°C/375°F/Gas Mark 5. Line a baking sheet with parchment paper.

Sift the flour into a mound, make a well in the centre and add the sugar, egg, egg yolk, butter, cream of tartar, bicarbonate of soda (baking soda) mixed with a little water and lemon zest. Mix to an even dough.

Taking small pieces of dough at a time, make little rolls, then flatten them and cut into diamond shapes. Put them on the prepared baking sheet and bake for about 15 minutes, until light golden brown. Remove from the oven.

Before decorating, preheat the oven to 180°C/350°F/Gas Mark 4, then turn off the heat.

Make the icing. Whisk the egg white with the lemon juice in a bowl, then stir in the icing (confectioners') sugar and mix well. Dip the biscuits (cookies) in the icing, put them on a baking sheet and dry in the oven with the door ajar.

BISCOTTINI ALLA GIUGGIULENA

Preparation time: 30 minutes
Cooking time: 15 minutes
Makes 30–40

Sesame seed biscuits (cookies)

- 500 g/1 lb 2 oz (4 cups) plain (all-purpose) flour
- 200 g/7 oz (1 cup) lard
- 200 g/7 oz (1 cup) caster (superfine) sugar
- 1 egg yolk
- grated zest of 1 lemon
- 1 teaspoon Marsala
- 2 teaspoons milk
- 5 tablespoons sesame seeds

Preheat the oven to 180°C/350°F/Gas Mark 4. Line 1–2 baking sheets with parchment paper.

Sift the flour into a mound on a work counter and make a well in the centre. Add the lard, sugar, egg yolk, lemon zest, Marsala and milk to the well and mix to an even dough.

Put the sesame seeds into a shallow dish. Shape small pieces of the dough into rolls the size of a little finger, roll them in the sesame seeds to coat and put them on the prepared baking sheet(s). Bake for 10–15 minutes, until very lightly coloured. Remove from the oven and transfer to a wire rack to cool. Store in an airtight container.

V

MESSINA

Poking out of the northeastern corner of the island, Messina is the third-largest city and capital of the province of Messina. It is usually the first stop for visitors coming from the mainland, especially if they are on their way to the Aeolian Islands. It has always been an important commercial and military port on the Straits of Messina.

Previous page:
The sun sets over the Strait of Messina, mainland Italy can be seen in the distance.

The cuisine of Messina can be summed up in a single word: seafood, and the protagonist of that is *pesce spada*, swordfish. Even though it can be found in other parts of the island's surrounding waters, the straits between Messina and the Calabria mainland are very fertile grounds for the swordfish. Interesting traditional fishing methods still survive, described below, and a wealth of recipes – although it is at its best simply grilled. Albacore, which belongs to the same family as swordfish, is also caught in the straits and in the Aeolian Islands, where it is cooked with tomatoes, capers and olives to make a traditional dish called *alalunga a ghiotta* ('greedy' swordfish).

The strait is the meeting point of the Tyrrhenian and Ionian seas, and provides a great variety of seafood. Fishermen still fish with *cannizzi*, woven palm fronds that float on the surface of the water, attracting fish to the shady surface. Dolphin fish are one of the species that can be collected in this way. Don't be alarmed if you see menus that list dolphin, these are not the much-loved mammal, but rather *Coryphaenna hippurus,* a warm water fish that can grow up to a metre (3 feet) long, also called *pisci capuni*, *paunissa*, *capuni* or *lampuga* in Sicilian. Sardines are abundant and used to make two favourite dishes: *sarde allinguate*, which are filleted and marinated in vinegar, then dredged in flour and fried, and *sarde chini o sucu*, which are filleted sardines sandwiched with a breadcrumb stuffing and tied together, then browned and simmered in tomato sauce.

The volcanic string of Aeolian Islands (Lipari, Salina, Stromboli, Filicudi, Alicudi, Panarea, Vulcano) provides romance and a serene, simple cuisine that can include lobster and copious amounts of capers and Malvasia wine. Don't miss the *caper sagra* on Salina the first weekend of June every year. It is like a potluck dinner, with every woman on the island bringing her caper speciality dish.

Deeper waters yield several important fish brought in with nets and long lines – mullet and cod (hake), for example. Cod has become a staple due to its abundance and mild flavour. Two methods of conservation, drying and salting, have long been used by fishermen and sailors to preserve it. The dried version is called stockfish, or piscistoccu, and the salted one is called *baccalà*. While *baccalà* is more traditional in Palermo, stockfish is more at home in Messina, cooked *a ghiotta* (with a briny condiment of tomatoes, olives and capers) or simply simmered with potatoes and tomatoes. Another preparation is known as *ventri i piscistoccu chini*, in which it is stuffed with breadcrumbs and cooked in tomato sauce. An alternative species of fish found in deep waters is the scabbard fish, known in Italian as *spatola*. A long, skinny fish, when filleted it is made into a popular dish filled with a breadcrumb stuffing and rolled up.

It's not all seafood in Messina province. The lovely, natural inland areas produce great meats and cheeses. The *provola sfoglia* is a unique cows' milk stretched-curd cheese that is sometimes made with a tiny green lemon inside, adding aromatic perfumes to the finished cheese; a very special meat is the delicious breed of pig from the Nebrodi park; and capers from the island of Salina are exceptional. Sweet-and-sour Nebrodi rabbit takes advantage of autumn (fall) flavours such as apple and hazelnuts. A lean meat like rabbit needs to cook in plenty of liquid to keep it tender, in this case a light broth flavoured with a spoonful of tomato purée (paste) called *'stratto*. Vinegar also helps tenderize a lean meat. The sweetness of the apple is juxtaposed with the tart vinegar to create an *agrodolce* (sweet and sour)

Following pages:
Messina's landscape is largely mountainous and comprises parts of both the Nebrodi and Peloritani mountain ranges. The combination of craggy peaks and deep waters make for a dramatic coastline.

flavour. Also on the table you will find elaborate meat dishes such as *farsumagru* (page 168), a rolled veal, egg and sausagemeat dish, and *pasta 'ncasciata* (page 162), a timbale layered with hearty ragù, boiled eggs, tiny meatballs, peas, salami, caciocavallo and sliced aubergine (eggplant): one of those labour-intensive but fabulously satisfying dishes. The word *'ncasciata* means 'encased', and it is often prepared with a final layer of fried aubergine encasing the dish with a dome over the layers, and is a recipe that varies from home to home. Vegetables are rich, varied and simply prepared.

The area is also known for some unique desserts, such as *pignolata glassata*, a pinecone-shaped soft biscuit (cookie) glazed on one half with lemon, and on the other half with chocolate. *Mustazzoli*, a sweet made from almonds, cinnamon, and cloves are attributed to Messina, and don't miss *riso nero*, sweet cooked rice made 'black' with chocolate and seasoned with nuts and candied fruit. Another specialty is *pasta reale di Tortorici*, similar to marzipan (page 89), but made with toasted hazelnuts instead of blanched almonds.

Though the area is known primarily for its seafood, Messina is also home to some of the Sicily's most famous meat dishes.

SALSA SALMORIGLIO

This sauce goes well with fish, particularly swordfish. The lemon juice can be replaced with a little vinegar for meat dishes.

Salmoriglio sauce

Preparation time: 15 minutes
Serves 4

- 200 ml/7 fl oz (scant 1 cup) olive oil
- juice of 2 lemons, strained
- 1 sprig oregano, chopped
- 1 sprig parsley, chopped
- salt and pepper

Pour the oil into a bowl and beat vigorously with a whisk, gradually adding the lemon juice, 1 tablespoon hot water, the oregano and parsley. Season to taste with salt and pepper.

SWORDFISH

Every year from April to October, the *pesce spada* (swordfish) populates the Straits of Messina. The ancient tradition of harpoon fishing is re-enacted from the special boats, *feluche*, which are equipped with a high lookout and long gangway at the bow. The swordfish returns to this spot every year to mate, and many also meet their fate here. Normally keeping to the depths of the sea, they come to the surface during this time, and the usually agile animal becomes quite slow and clumsy, making it very easy to be harpooned and brought in.

The easiest preparations are the best, such as simply grilled steaks with *salmoriglio* or *sammurigghiu*, a condiment served with grilled (broiled) meats or seafood or tuna. It is made with lemon juice, olive oil, garlic, oregano, parsley and salt and pepper. Also found in other parts of Sicily, it has several variations, including a refreshing one in Catania called *agghiata*, which uses mint and vinegar instead of lemon. Back in Messina, *agghiata* is a local name for *ghiotta*, a fresh sauce of tomatoes, olives and capers, which is also splendid with swordfish. In its classic preparation, the best-quality steak from the breast is roasted in the oven and covered with a rich *ghiotta* of onions, green olives, pine nuts, celery, tomatoes, bay leaves, raisins, capers, sometimes potatoes... and, of course, olive oil. A bit more complex, but still simple, are Messina-style stuffed swordfish rolls with olives, tomatoes, anchovy and red chilli (page 156), as is *ruota di pesce spada* (page 158), swordfish baked with potato and saffron, cherry tomatoes, capers, onion and mint.

The deep waters of the Strait of Messina are home to formidable-looking swordfish for much of the year. The fish have become synonymous with Sicilian cuisine and feature in many of the island's most-iconic dishes.

INVOLTINI DI SPADA ALLA MESSINESE

Messina-style swordfish rolls

Preparation time: 45 minutes
Cooking time: 35 minutes
Serves 6

- 12 thin slices of swordfish, about 1 kg/2¼ lb, skinned
- 70 g/2¾ oz (scant ¾ cup) grated caciocavallo cheese
- 2 tablespoons breadcrumbs
- 2 tablespoons chopped flat-leaf parsley
- 2 sprigs basil, chopped
- olive oil, for drizzling
- salt and pepper

For the sauce

- 1 celery stalk
- 1 small onion
- 8–9 ripe tomatoes, peeled, seeded and diced
- 2 tablespoons olive oil
- 2 tablespoons capers preserved in salt, rinsed
- 100 g/3½ oz (1 cup) pitted Gaeta olives, halved
- salt

Trim the swordfish slices to make neat rectangles, reserving the trimmings. Cover each rectangle with clingfilm (plastic wrap) and beat lightly with the side of a rolling pin, being careful not to break the flesh.

Chop the trimmings and mix them with the grated cheese, breadcrumbs, parsley and basil in a bowl. Drizzle with olive oil, season with salt and pepper and mix again.

Lay the fish slices on the work counter and divide the filling among them, then roll up and secure with wooden cocktail sticks or toothpicks.

Make the sauce. Blanch the celery in salted boiling water for 3–4 minutes, then drain and slice. Pour water into a pan to a depth of 1.5 cm/¾ inch, add a pinch of salt and the onion and cook over low heat for 15–20 minutes, until the onion is softened and translucent. Add the tomatoes, oil, capers, olives and celery and simmer, stirring occasionally, for 15 minutes.

Add the swordfish rolls to the pan of sauce, cover and cook for another 10 minutes. Lift off the lid, remove and discard the cocktail sticks or toothpicks and cook for a few minutes more. Remove the pan from the heat and serve the rolls hot or cold with the sauce spooned over them.

RUOTA DI PESCE SPADA

Baked Swordfish

Preparation time: 20 minutes
Cooking time: 40 minutes
Serves 6

- 1 × 900-g/2-lb swordfish steak, a maximum of 6 cm/2½ inches thick, cut from the belly
- 200 ml/7 fl oz (scant 1 cup) olive oil
- 1–1½ teaspoons chilli flakes
- juice of 2 lemons
- 2 cloves garlic, chopped
- 1 bunch of parsley, chopped
- twists of lemon zest, to garnish
- salt

Preheat the oven to 160°C/325°F/Gas Mark 3 and put a roasting pan filled with water in the bottom. Line a baking sheet a little larger than the fish with foil, letting the sides overhang. Generously brush the foil with some of the oil, sprinkle with a pinch each of chilli flakes and salt, drizzle with 2 tablespoons lemon juice and sprinkle with some of the the garlic and parsley.

Put the fish on top. Drizzle the remaining oil and lemon juice over the surface and around the outside and sprinkle with the remaining chilli flakes, garlic, parsley and a pinch of salt. Fold over the foil to make a package and bake for 40 minutes.

Remove the baking sheet from the oven and carefully open the package. Transfer the fish to a warm serving dish, garnish with twists of lemon peel and cut into vertical slices like a cake.

PESCESTOCCO ALLA MESSINESE

Messina-style cod

Preparation time: 20 minutes
Cooking time: 1 hour
Serves 6

- 1 kg/2¼ lb plum tomatoes, preferably San Marzano, chopped
- 100 ml/3½ fl oz (scant ½ cup) olive oil
- 1 onion, chopped
- 100 g/3½ oz (1 cup) celery, thinly sliced
- 1 kg/2¼ lb stockfish (unsalted dried cod or other white fish), soaked in several changes of water for 48 hours and drained
- 50 g/2 oz (scant ½ cup) capers
- 100 g/3½ oz (1 cup) pitted green olives in brine
- 1 kg/2¼ lb potatoes, cut into sticks
- salt and cayenne pepper

Put the tomatoes into a shallow dish and let stand until their liquid has evaporated. Press the tomatoes through a nylon sieve (strainer) into a bowl.

Heat the oil in a flameproof dish, add the onion and cook over low heat, stirring occasionally, for 5 minutes, until softened and translucent. Add the celery and strained tomatoes and bring to a boil, Meanwhile, cut the fish into large pieces. Add the fish, capers, olives and potatoes to the dish, season with salt and cayenne pepper and simmer for 40–50 minutes. Remove from the heat and let stand for a few minutes, then transfer to a warmed serving dish and serve.

PASTA 'NCASCIATA

Baked pasta

Preparation time: 1 hour 30 minutes + standing time
Cooking time: 20 minutes
Serves 6

- 3 aubergines (eggplants), sliced into rounds
- 2 eggs
- 150 ml/¼ pint (⅔ cup) vegetable oil
- 4 tablespoons olive oil
- 1 clove garlic, peeled
- 600 g/1 lb 5 oz ripe tomatoes, peeled and chopped
- 5 basil leaves
- 80 g/3 oz ham, finely chopped
- 80 g/3 oz lean beef, finely chopped
- 80 g/3 oz chicken livers, trimmed and finely chopped
- butter, for greasing
- 4–6 tablespoons fresh breadcrumbs
- 425 g/15 oz maccheroni
- 80 g/3 oz mozzarella cheese, diced
- 25 g/1 oz (⅓ cup) grated pecorino cheese
- salt and pepper

Put the aubergine (eggplant) slices into a colander, sprinkling each layer with salt and let stand for 30 minutes. Meanwhile, cook the eggs in lightly salted boiling water for 8–10 minutes until hard-boiled. Remove from the heat, rinse under cold running water, shell and cut into wedges.

Rinse the aubergine slices and pat dry with paper towels. Heat the vegetable oil in a large frying pan or skillet, add the aubergine slices, in batches, and cook until golden brown on both sides. Drain on paper towels and set aside.

Heat the olive oil in a shallow pan, add the garlic clove and cook over low heat, stirring frequently, for a few minutes, until lightly browned, then remove and discard it. Add the tomatoes and basil to the pan and cook, stirring, for a few minutes, then add the ham, beef and chicken livers. Increase the heat to medium, season, cover and cook for 20 minutes.

Preheat the oven to 180°C/350°F/Gas Mark 4. Grease a deep ovenproof dish large enough to hold the pasta with butter and sprinkle with the breadcrumbs, shaking out the excess. Bring a large pan of salted water to a boil, add the pasta, bring back to a boil and cook for 8–10 minutes, or according to the package instructions, until al dente. Drain and return to the pan, then pour the meat sauce over it. Add the mozzarella, hard-boiled eggs and aubergines, stir and pour into the prepared dish. Sprinkle with the pecorino and bake for 20 minutes. Remove the dish from the oven and let stand for a few minutes, then turn out onto a warmed serving dish to serve.

SALUMI

As with most of Italy, cured pork products are very popular in Sicily. Other, less conventional, meats, such as tuna, are also cured here.

Salumi is the generic term for cured meats, from prosciutto to small air-dried sausages. The production of cured meats in Sicily started after the departure of the Saracens, who did not consume pork products. As in other parts of Italy, the salting and drying of meats was a safe way to preserve protein. Cured meats are divided into two categories: whole cuts of meat, such as the leg for prosciutto or loin, and meats cured in casings (*insaccato*), called *salame* individually. The most commonly used meat is pork, although there are some products from other meats, such as *ficazza* made from tuna.

The procedure always involves salt, because the salt is what draws out the moisture and allows the meat to be preserved, and air-drying. Unlike other parts of Italy, the climate in the south was much too hot to allow large pieces such as prosciutto to cure. The tradition was to create smaller pieces of chopped or whole meats that could dry quickly and safely. Now that there is refrigeration, though, larger pieces can be cured; the hind leg is destined for prosciutto. Some traditional *salumi* include *lonza* (loin), *lardo* (cured fat), *pancetta* (cured belly), dried sausages, and salami in various shapes and sizes.

The meat used in *salumi* is very important. Especially prized is the Nebrodi Black Pig, a small semi-feral animal similar to the wild boar. The meat is eaten fresh or cured and is sold from October to April. *Salame di Sant'Angelo* is one of the products that uses the Nebrodi Black Pig. Made in Sant'Angelo di Brolo, it contains 20 per cent fat and hand-cut chunks of pork from the best parts. *Fellata* is another *salame* from San Marco, made from the better cuts of the Nebrodi black pig. The fat comes from the pancetta and is mixed with the chopped meat and seasoned with salt, pepper, and sometimes chilli, put into casings and aged for up to three months.

Following pages:
Messina's inland areas are renowned for the production of good-quality meat and cow's milk cheeses.

FARSUMAGRU

Stuffed meat

Preparation time: 30 minutes
Cooking time: 1 hour 25 minutes
Serves 6–8

- 1 × 700–800-g/1½ lb–1¾-lb boneless slice of veal
- 300 g/11 oz minced (ground) veal
- 2 tablespoons breadcrumbs
- 50 g/2 oz (½ cup) grated caciocavallo cheese
- 50 g/2 oz (⅔ cup) grated pecorino cheese
- 1 egg, plus 1 egg yolk
- 3 tablespoons chopped flat-leaf parsley, plus extra to garnish
- 100 g/3½ oz) salami, sliced
- 3 hard-boiled eggs, shelled
- 2 tablespoons olive oil
- 4 tablespoons dry white wine
- 1 small onion, sliced
- 2 tablespoons tomato purée (paste)
- salt and pepper

Lay the slice of veal on a board, cover with clingfilm (plastic wrap) and beat with a meat mallet or the side of a rolling pin to a thickness of about 1 cm/½ inch, then discard the clingfilm. Mix together the minced (ground) veal, breadcrumbs, caciocavallo, pecorino, egg, egg yolk and parsley in a bowl and season with salt and pepper. Spread the mixture evenly over the slice of veal, then cover with the slices of salami and put the whole hard-boiled eggs on top. Roll up and tie with kitchen string. Heat 1 tablespoon of the oil in a frying pan or skillet, add the roll and cook over medium heat, turning occasionally, for 7–8 minutes, until evenly browned. Drizzle in the wine and cook until the alcohol has evaporated, then transfer the roll to a flameproof casserole (Dutch oven).

Heat a few tablespoons of water with a pinch of salt in a small shallow pan, add the onion and cook over medium heat until the liquid has evaporated. Add the remaining oil and cook, stirring occasionally, for 7–10 minutes, until lightly browned, then transfer to the casserole. Mix the tomato purée (paste) with a little water, add to the casserole, cover and cook for 1 hour, drizzling with hot water if required.

Remove the casserole from the heat, lift out the meat and let stand for 5 minutes. Remove the string, cut the roll into slices and put them onto a serving dish. Pour the cooking juices, reduced if necessary, over the meat, garnish with parsley and serve hot or cold.

GRANITA

Native to Sicily, the granita is known and emulated the world over. Granita in Sicily comes in a huge variety of flavours and each region has its own specialty.

The famous Italian granita originated in Sicily and its roots can be found in the flavoured ice 'sherbets' that found their way to Sicily during the Arab occupation. It is said that the first Sicilian granitas were made from the snow that lay on the peaks of Mount Etna and the Nebrodi mountains.

Similar to a sorbet, but with a much grainier consistency, the traditional flavour and texture of the dish varies throughout the island. In Catania it is very common to find granita flavoured with almonds, whereas in Messina it is often flavoured with coffee and served with cream (page 172).

GRANITA DI CAFFÈ

Coffee granita

Preparation time: 10 minutes + 2 hours freezing
Serves 6

- 140 g/5 oz (⅔ cup) caster (superfine) sugar
- 1.5 litres/2½ pints (6¼ cups) extra strong coffee
- 250 ml/8 fl oz (1 cup) whipping cream or double (heavy) cream, whipped

Heat the sugar with 500 ml/18 fl oz (generous 2 cups) water in a pan over a low heat until dissolved. Add the coffee, stir and set aside until completely cooled.

Pour the mixture into a freezer-proof container and place in the freezer for 2 hours or just over, stirring every 20 minutes to give it a granular texture. Serve in dishes or glasses and decorate with whipped cream.

DOLCETTI CON PASTA REALE DI TORTORICI

Sweets with Tortorici marzipan

A traditional festive sweet treat from Tortorici, a village in the Monti Nebrodi, where hazelnuts were once one of the most common crops.

Preparation time: 35 minutes + 12 hours standing
Cooking time: 20 minutes
Serves 8

- 1 kg/2¼ lb (9 cups) shelled hazelnuts
- 1.2 kg/2½ lb (6 cups) caster (superfine) sugar
- plain (all-purpose) flour, for dusting
- butter, for greasing
- icing (confectioners') sugar, for dusting

Preheat the oven to 180°C/350°F/Gas Mark 4. Spread the nuts on a baking sheet and toast in the oven for 15–20 minutes. Remove from the oven and tip onto a clean dish towel. Rub them vigorously with the dish towel to remove the skins, then chop coarsely.

Put them into a bowl, add the sugar and mix with very little water. Shape small amounts of the mixture into golf ball-size balls. Lightly dust the palm of one hand with flour, take a hazelnut ball and pinch it with the thumb, index and middle fingers of the other hand to leave an imprint in the dough. Put the balls on a lightly floured dish towel and let stand for 12 hours.

Preheat the oven to 160°C/325°F/Gas mark 3. Grease an ovenproof dish with butter and transfer the hazelnut balls to it, arranging them in a single layer. Bake for about 20 minutes, until they are browned and puffy in the centres. Remove from the oven, let cool and then dust with icing (confectioners') sugar.

VI

ENNA

Enna was founded by one of the indigenous tribes in 1200 BC. Mythology has it that it was in the Valley of Enna – perhaps at Lake Pergusa – that Persephone (known to Italians as Proserpina) was abducted by Hades, causing her mother Demeter, the goddess of agriculture, to despair, which resulted in a famine for the mortals. Persephone's father Zeus intervened and made Persephone the goddess of wheat, but Hades had a hold on her that required her to return to him four months out of the year. Those months became the unproductive season for the wheat.

In the first century BC, the Romans exploited Enna, and Sicily in general. Under the Romans, the forests disappeared to become warships, and the land became vast wheat fields to feed Rome. Deforestation has had an enormous effect on the climate of Sicily, leading to decline of rainfall and drying up of rivers. Unprotected by the forest cover, land erodes; flooding follows and the water is not absorbed. The Roman engineers did not interest themselves in the consequences of their actions. They knew how to farm, fertilize and rotate crops, but they did not understand the effects of interfering with the natural environment.

Wheat continues to be an important crop today. The wheat grown here is a hard grain, high in protein, called *semola* (semolina). It is ideal for making dried pasta, and local bakers also use it for bread, such as the *pagnotte di Enna*, a bread made with 100 per cent semolina flour. Many traditions evolve around bread, often in connection with religious rituals. Every September, in honour of the harvest, the small agricultural town of Catenanuova hosts the annual festival of grain.

The province of Enna is intensely agricultural. As well as wheat, the fertile hills provide an abundance of vegetables and pulses (legumes). In the spring, artichokes are stuffed with garlic, onion, parsley and grated cheese.

Previous page:
Wild garlic grows on a hilltop overlooking the patchwork of fields that form the Enna landscape.

In the twelfth century, at the behest of the Norman king Roger, Enna and Piazza Armerina began to produce a unique, aged pecorino (a sheeps' milk cheese) called *piacentinu*, which is flavoured with saffron and pepper. The Sicilian dialect name means 'enjoyable'. King Roger believed that saffron had an anti-depressant effect, and exotic peppercorns were added because he loved the flavour. Saffron has grown in the area since the Middle ages. Each bulb produces a maximum of 12 crimson stigmas (the part of a the female pistil that receives the pollen during pollination), making it one of the world's most costly spices by weight.

When making the *piacentinu*, 5 grams (¼ ounce) saffron is added to each 100 litres (26 gallons) of milk. The saffron is passed and re-passed through the milk with sieves (strainers) several times to ensure maximum flavour and colour. Once cooked, the whole black peppercorns are added, the cheese is drained and shaped, salted and aged for several months. As well as the *piacentinu* cheese, you will also find saffron in local dishes, such as pasta with cauliflower or fennel, saffron and salted sardines. Interestingly, Bartolomeo Scappi's *Opera dell'arte del Cucinare*, published in 1570, states that pasta was often cooked in broth, with rose water, saffron and cinnamon among the typical spices used.

Nearby in Leonforte, a special peach is grown that has achieved DOP (protected geographical status), celebrated on the first Sunday of October in a local festival. Leonforte is also home to a broad (fava) bean that has been recognized by Slow Food. Once a rotation crop for wheat, even in Roman times, the Leonforte broad bean is used frequently in the traditional local kitchen. Still cultivated by hand, when harvested they are dried in small bunches (*manate di favi*) and threshed to separate the stalks and leaves from the bean. A favourite dish is *maccu*, a purée of cooked beans.

Following pages:
Piazza Armerina is one of Enna's most-popular tourist destinations, it is notable for its well-preserved Roman mosaics, which can be found at the Villa Romana del Casale.

MELANZANE A BECCAFICO

Stuffed aubergine (eggplant) slices

Preparation time: 30 minutes + 1 hour salting
Cooking time: 20 minutes
Serves 4

- 2 tablespoons raisins
- 12 aubergine (eggplant) slices
- olive oil, for brushing
- 40 g/1½ oz (⅔ cup) fresh white breadcrumbs
- 2–3 tablespoons pine nuts
- 12 bay leaves
- lemon juice, to serve
- coarse salt

Put the raisins into a small bowl, pour in water to cover and let soak. Put the aubergine (eggplant) slices into a bowl of water mixed with coarse salt and let soak for 1 hour, then drain, squeeze out and spread out on a dish towel.

Make the stuffing. Heat a frying pan or skillet and brush with olive oil. Add the breadcrumbs and toast over medium-low heat, stirring frequently, for a few minutes, until golden. Transfer the crumbs to a bowl and add the pine nuts. Drain the raisins, squeeze out, add to the bowl and mix well.

Preheat the oven to 180°C/350°F/Gas Mark 4. Put a little filling on each aubergine slice, fold into a half-moon shape and put them into an ovenproof dish with a bay leaf between each roll. Bake for 10 minutes, then remove from the oven. Serve hot or cold lightly drizzled with lemon juice.

PASTA

Enna is known for the production of wheat and its markets are home to an abundance of pasta in all of its forms.

Cato described Enna as 'the Republic's granary, the nurse at whose breast the Roman people are fed.' The fact remains true today, but the market has grown much larger. Much of the pasta produced in Italy is made with grain grown in Sicily. The grain is *semola* (semolina), a hard wheat with high protein levels and the potential to develop gluten, which gives the dough its elasticity. Once harvested, the wheat must be cleaned to remove any foreign material and imperfect grains. It is then tempered – a method of controlling the moisture content – to allow easier separation of the bran and the germ. At this point the grain can be milled for flour with repeated grinding and sifting.

The golden semolina flour is best adapted for dried pasta, or *pasta asciutta*, which has two versions, artisanal or industrial. The major distinctions between the two are the type of extrusion method and the temperature and time of the drying. Both versions are made with semolina flour and water. The artisanal method involves extrusion from bronze dies, perforated with the desired shape, whereas industrial methods use Teflon. The bronze gives a rugged texture to the pasta that helps hold the sauce, and Teflon, while easier to clean and much longer lasting, makes a pasta that is very smooth on the outside. The major difference is the way it is dried. In an industrial setting, the pasta is dried at high temperatures very quickly. Artisanal producers use a slow, ventilated drying method at very low temperatures. This low temperature method helps retain the flavour and nutritional value of the wheat.

Following pages:
A freshly harvested field of golden wheat, one of many that makes up Enna's distinctly agricultural landscape.

Some favourite shapes are spaghetti, anelletti (little rings), hand-made gnocculi (cannelloni) and gnucchitti (small, ridged tubes), cavateddi (cavatelli, or small shells), and ditalini (short tubes).

RUOTE AL SUGO DI SALSICCIA

Pasta wheels with sausage sauce

Preparation time: 15 minutes
Cooking time: 1 hour 30 minutes
Serves 4

- 400 g/14 oz pasta wheels (rotelle)
- 50 g/2 oz (⅔ cup) grated piacentino or Parmesan cheese
- salt

For the sauce

- 2 tablespoons olive oil
- 3 Italian sausages, casings removed
- 1 celery stalk, finely chopped
- 1 carrot, finely chopped
- 1 onion, finely chopped
- 300–400 g/11–14 oz (1¼–1⅔ cups) tomato sauce or 3 tablespoons tomato purée (paste)
- 1 bay leaf
- pinch of ground cinnamon
- 1 clove
- pinch of freshly grated nutmeg
- 200 ml/7 fl oz (scant 1 cup) red wine
- salt and pepper

First, make the sauce. Heat the oil in a shallow pan and add the sausage meat, breaking it up with a wooden spoon. Cook over medium low heat, turning occasionally, for a few minutes, until golden brown, then remove from the pan. Add the celery, carrot and onion to the pan, reduce the heat to low and cook, stirring occasionally, for 5 minutes, until softened. Stir in the tomato sauce, if using, or mix the tomato purée (paste) with a little water and stir into the pan. Return the sausage meat to the pan, add the bay leaf, cinnamon, clove and nutmeg, season with a pinch each of salt and pepper, drizzle with the wine and cook until the alcohol has evaporated.

Pour in water to cover and simmer over very low heat, stirring occasionally and adding a little more water, if necessary, for 1 hour, until the sauce has thickened. Remove and discard the bay leaf.

Bring a large pan of salted water to a boil, add the pasta, bring back to a boil and cook for about 10 minutes, or according to package instructions, until al dente. Remove from the heat, drain and tip onto a serving dish. Add the sauce and toss lightly. Serve immediately, handing the grated cheese separately.

PORK

Traditionally, large pieces of meat, such as these prosciutto, could not be produced in Sicily because of the warm climate; modern refrigeration techniques have now made this possible.

Apart from the two hundred years when the island was under Arab control, pork has long been the first choice of meat. Two heirloom breeds are considered indigenous in Sicily: the Black Pig of Nebrodi (*suino nero dei Nebrodi*) and the Black Pig of the Madonie (*suino nero delle Madonie*). The pigs are generally black in colour, but due to some inbreeding, they are sometimes coloured with both black and white. They are half wild, raised free range in the forested areas of the two mountainous regions at the north side of the island. Their presence dates back at least to the Greek period. Other breeds have been introduced to enhance commercial success, and due to the diminished forested areas the black breeds were nearly phased out. Some producers realized that the quality of their meat was more valuable than the quantity produced by the new breeds and initiated a return to the original breeds for the best flavour. Studies have also show them to be commercially viable, because they are stronger than domestic breeds, have better longevity, and produce more offspring. Today there is a resurgence in numbers and an appreciation for their products.

When the pig is butchered, the prime cuts for curing are cut and set aside. Next, the chops and steaks that will be eaten fresh are prepared. After that, all the small scraps and fat are used to create various *salumi* (page 165). Small pieces of the prime cuts are also used to make fresh sausages, usually with about 30 per cent high-quality fat from the belly. Seasonings are simple: salt, pepper, spicy dried chillies, garlic, fennel seeds and wild fennel. Usually eaten grilled or cooked with vegetables, one of the specialties of Nicosia is *budello origanato*, a sausage made of minced (ground) pork and rabbit.

Following pages:
The Black Pigs of Nebrodi are unique to Sicily and their meat is highly prized.

SALSICCIA AL FINOCCHIETTO ARANCE E PANE

Fennel sausages with oranges and bread

Finocchietto, finocchiella or wild fennel is a widely used aromatic herb for flavouring meat and fish dishes and mixed grills (broils) throughout southern Italy. It goes very well with lamb and, in Sicily, it is used in sausage products.

Preparation time: 20 minutes
Cooking time: 1 hour
Serves 6

- 10–12 fennel-flavoured Italian sausages
- 100 ml/3½ fl oz (scant ½ cup) dry white wine
- 3–4 oranges
- 3–4 tablespoons olive oil
- 6 slices rustic bread

Prick the sausages with the tip of a sharp knife, put them into a shallow pan, set over medium-high heat and cook, turning occasionally, for a few minutes until evenly browned. Drizzle with the wine and cook until the alcohol has evaporated, then reduce the heat, cover and cook, turning occasionally, for about 1 hour. Add a little water if the sausages are becoming too dry.

Meanwhile, peel the oranges, removing all traces of bitter white pith, then slice. Heat 3 tablespoons of the oil in a frying pan or skillet. Add the bread slices, in batches, and cook over medium heat, turning once, for a few minutes until browned on both sides. Remove with a fish slice (spatula), cut in half and drain on paper towels. Add more oil to the pan if necessary for another batch.

Divide the sausages, orange slices and bread among 6 plates. Serve this extremely delicious and aromatic dish before the sausages become too cool. It is tastier hot or still warm.

SFINCI

Sweet fritters with citrus syrup

Preparation time: 1 hour 15 minutes
Cooking time: 30 minutes
Makes about 24 fritters

- 1 tablespoon lard
- 1½ teaspoons caster (superfine) sugar
- 250 g/9 oz (2¼ cups) plain (all-purpose) flour, plus extra for dusting
- 6 eggs
- grated zest of 1 lemon
- 1 litre/1¾ pints (4¼ cups) vegetable oil, plus extra for brushing
- ground cinnamon, for dusting
- salt

For the syrup

- 300 g/11 oz (1½ cups) caster (superfine) sugar
- grated zest of 1 lemon
- grated zest of 1 orange

First make the dough. Pour 300 ml/½ pint (1¼ cups) water into a pan, add the lard, sugar and a pinch of salt and bring to a boil. Remove the pan from the heat, add all the flour at once and beat well. Return the pan to the heat and cook, stirring constantly, until the mixture comes away from the side of the pan. Remove from the heat and let cool. When the mixture is cold, beat in the eggs, 1 at a time, then mix in the lemon zest. Turn out the dough onto a lightly floured surface and knead vigorously.

Heat the oil in a deep-fryer to 180°C/350°F or until a cube of bread browns in 30 seconds. Brush your hand and the handle of a wooden spoon with oil. Take a small portion of the dough and shape it into a ball. Make a hole in the middle with the handle of the oiled spoon and slide it into the hot oil. Continue making sfinci in this way, brushing your hand and the spoon handle with oil as required. Cook a few at a time, turning them frequently until golden brown. Remove with a slotted spoon, drain on paper towels and let cool.

Meanwhile make the syrup. Pour 300 ml/½ pint (1¼ cups) water into a pan, preferably a copper one, add the sugar and stir until it has completely dissolved. Bring to a boil and cook until the temperature measures 105°C/225°F on a sugar (candy) thermometer and the mixture is slightly thickened and syrupy. Remove the pan from the heat and let cool slightly, then stir in the lemon and orange zest. Dip the sfinci in the syrup, arrange them on a serving dish and let cook completely. Dust with cinnamon and serve.

VII

CATANIA

Mount Etna, the tallest active European volcano, dominates life in Catania. A constant reminder on the skyline, with an ever-present plume of smoke drifting up to the sky, it commands a reverent, careful respect. Even in the face of imminent danger, the fertile land is irresistible for everything from blood oranges, nuts and prickly pears (*fichi d'india*), to grapes for wine. Its hard, lava-sculpted surfaces are not easy to farm, with a dark swirling landscape and snow in the upper elevations, and small huts built of volcanic material on the lower slopes; but they are rich with iron. Intense flavours erupt from the garlic and kid of Randazzo, the sweet cherries from Macchia and Bronte's pistachios. There is no shortage of honey, almonds and chestnuts, and good grapes grow on the northern slopes. East and along the coast is one of Sicily's largest citrus zones, especially known for the blood orange juicing varieties called Moro and Sanguinello. Beyond Mount Etna is the Nebrodi Natural Park, which is home to half of Sicily's total forested area. The mountains are alive with wildlife, streams and natural wonders. Of the eighteen municipalities within the park, three belong to the province of Catania.

Previous page:
The Amenano fountain at the entrance of Catania's bustling fish market.

In the city of Catania, although the roots are ancient, the Baroque architecture is not. The entire city was destroyed in 1693 by earthquakes, and it has been covered in lava seven times, each time built anew. Fera o Luni, the largest market, is held every morning in Piazza Carlo Alberto with a backdrop of regal buildings. Here fresh produce from the countryside can be found, as well as olives seasoned with spicy chillies, roasted chickpeas, meat and fresh fish.

The fish market at the Piazza Duomo is one of the island's most colourful and lively, and Catania's oldest market. Seventy kilometres (40 miles) of coastline provide an array of sea creatures trembling with freshness, from tiny sea snails to octopus, swordfish, sea urchins (*riccio di mare*), hard-shell clams and squid, to name a few.

Though the town of Catania has been damaged by earthquakes and eruptions from Etna, and rebuilt many times, a few buildings, such as this church, have withstood the forces of nature.

Two different types of squid can be found in Sicily. White calamari from the southern seas are tender and delicate in flavour, and totani from the north and eastern seas are red with a stronger flavour. Both are delicious stuffed, breaded, stewed or grilled (broiled). Different varieties of octopus are found everywhere, from fine restaurants to food stands selling them from large pots. In the same category of cephalopods, cuttlefish provide the black ink, *nero di seppia*, known as *u mungibeddu* in Catania, which is tossed with spaghetti and sprinkled with *ricotta salata* (salted ricotta), a symbol of Mount Etna.

Previous pages:
Anchovy fishermen brave the early morning off the coast of Catania. Mount Etna can just be seen through the dawn haze.

Street food in Catania has a slightly different take from that of Palermo. Although some similar foods, such as *arancini* (stuffed rice balls) can be found, stands and trucks sell sandwiches, *scacciate* (savoury dough pies) and *crespelle* (stuffed crêpes), and in the evenings large braziers roast various meats and fill the streets with their smoky aromas.

The 5th of February each year, the patron Saint Agatha is celebrated with a passionate festival. According to legend, the saint's breasts were cut off for refusing the advances of a Roman official. Small, breast-shaped cakes called *minne di St Agata* (St Agatha's breasts) are dedicated to her. Another dish is referenced to a religious source: San Bernardo sauce. This sauce is made with chocolate, almonds, anchovies, orange and vinegar, and takes its name from a monastery in Catania. It seems the monks in it were known to have a taste for rich foods.

Catanian food shows Sicilian cuisine making its most creative use of land and sea. The most famous dish is *pasta alla norma* (Norma-style Pasta), made with aubergines (eggplants) and tomatoes in the height of summer. Other favourites include *cozze pepate* (peppered mussels) and spaghetti with fresh sea urchins, and horsemeat is not uncommon.

The town of Randazzo at the foot of Mount Etna. The Church of Santa Maria (to the right of this photograph) is built entirely from black lava stone.

Following pages:
The town of Castiglione di Sicilia lies nestled in the hills that make up the Catania landscape.

ARANCINI

Stuffed rice balls

Preparation time: 2 hours
Cooking time: 30–40 minutes
Serves 6

- 300 g/11 oz (1½ cups) risotto rice
- 100 g/3½ oz (scant 1 cup) grated mature (sharp) caciocavallo cheese
- 150 g/5 oz mozzarella cheese, cut into cubes
- 2 eggs
- 80 g/3 oz (1¾ cups) fresh breadcrumbs
- olive or vegetable oil, for deep-frying
- salt

For the meat sauce

- 200 g/7 oz (1⅓ cups) shelled peas
- 40 g/1½ oz (3 tablespoons) butter
- 2 tablespoons olive oil
- ½ onion, chopped
- 250 g/9 oz minced (ground) steak
- 2 tablespoons dry white wine,
- 1 tablespoon tomato purée (paste)
- salt and pepper

Cook the rice in a large pan of salted boiling water for 15–20 minutes, until al dente, then drain. Transfer to a bowl, stir in the grated cheese and let cool.

Meanwhile, make the meat sauce. Blanch the peas in boiling water for 5 minutes, then drain and set aside. Melt the butter with the oil in a pan, add the onion and cook over low heat, stirring occasionally, for 5 minutes, until softened. Add the minced (ground) meat, increase the heat to medium and cook, stirring frequently, until lightly browned. Add the white wine and cook until the alcohol has evaporated, then mix the tomato purée (paste) with a little water in a small bowl and stir into the pan. Season to taste with salt and pepper, cover and simmer over low heat for 50 minutes. Add the peas, re-cover the pan and simmer for another 10 minutes.

Make the croquettes. Take a little rice and put it in the palm of your left hand, then shape it to resemble a small, slightly pointed orange with your right hand. Make a small hollow in the centre with your right thumb and fill with a teaspoon of meat sauce and a cube of soft cheese, then cover with the rice.

Beat the eggs with a pinch of salt in a shallow dish and spread out the breadcrumbs in another dish. Heat the oil in a deep-fryer to 180°C/350°F or until a cube of bread browns in 30 seconds. Dip the croquettes first in the beaten egg and then in the breadcrumbs to coat. Add them to the hot oil, in batches, and cook until lightly golden brown. Remove and drain on paper towels, then transfer to a warmed serving dish and keep hot while you cook the remaining batches. Serve hot.

AUBERGINES (EGGPLANTS)

It is speculated that aubergines (eggplants), locally known as *petronciana*, arrived with the Arabs, although were not fully accepted as edible until the sixteenth century. It quickly became one of Sicily's iconic ingredients. *Pasta alla Norma* (Norma-style Pasta), made with aubergine and tomato, is a classic Sicilian dish that originates in Catania. Some believe that the dish is named after the opera, *La Norma*, by the composer Vincenzo Bellini, who was born in Catania, but there are others who believe that the name refers to the Italian phrase *a norma*, meaning 'according to the rules specified in the recipe'. One of the key ingredients is *ricotta salata*: ricotta that has been pressed, salted and aged.

Caponata is another classic dish, and is found in all parts of Sicily. It truly represents the essence of Sicily – the ingredients of the sun and the historic influences. It is made with sautéed aubergine, tomato, celery, olives and onions, and dressed with a sweet-sour mixture of olive oil, vinegar and sugar, to which capers are added. A great number of variations exist, some including sweet peppers, pine nuts or raisins. Once prepared, the mixture is cooled and served at room temperature or chilled as an appetizer, or as an accompaniment to the meat course.

Vibrant aubergines (eggplants) for sale at a bustling Catania market. The aubergine forms the basis of many of Sicily's classic dishes.

CAPONATA CLASSICA

Classic caponata

Preparation time: 1 hour
Cooking time: 1 hour 40 minutes
Serves 4–6

- 150 ml/¼ pint (⅔ cup) olive oil
- 4 large round aubergines (eggplants), cut into cubes
- 1 onion, thinly sliced into rings
- 50–80 g/2–3 oz (¼–½ cup) sugar
- 400 g/14 oz (1⅔ cups) passata (puréed canned tomatoes)
- 100 ml/3½ fl oz (scant ½ cup) white wine vinegar
- 2 celery stalks, blanched and cut into small pieces
- 90 g/3 oz (⅔ cup) capers preserved in salt, rinsed in water acidulated with vinegar
- 150 g/5 oz (1½ cups) pitted green olives, blanched and chopped
- 3 tablespoons raisins, soaked in warm water for 10 minutes, drained and squeezed out
- 25 g/1 oz (¼ cup) pine nuts
- 1 sprig basil, shredded
- 50 g/2 oz (1 cup) fresh breadcrumbs
- 3 tablespoons blanched almonds, toasted and chopped
- salt

Heat 5 tablespoons of the oil in a frying pan or skillet, add the aubergines (eggplants) and cook, stirring frequently, for 10 minutes, until golden brown. Remove with a slotted spoon and drain on paper towels.

Heat 2 tablespoons of the remaining oil in a heavy-bottomed pan. Add the onion and cook over low heat, stirring occasionally, for 10 minutes, until golden, then stir in 3 tablespoons of the sugar and cook for another 10–20 minutes, until caramelized. Remove the pan from the heat.

Heat the passata (puréed canned tomatoes) in a small pan, then stir in the vinegar and remaining sugar. Heat 2 tablespoons of the remaining oil in a large frying pan or skillet, add the celery and caramelized onion and cook over low heat, stirring occasionally, for 5 minutes. Add the capers, olives, raisins and pine nuts and cook, stirring occasionally, for a few minutes, then stir in the tomato sauce mixture, basil and aubergines. Simmer for 15 minutes, then season to taste with salt and add more sugar if necessary. Remove the pan from the heat and transfer the caponata to a serving dish.

Heat the remaining oil in a small pan, add the breadcrumbs and cook over medium heat, stirring frequently, for a few minutes until golden brown. Remove from the heat and sprinkle them over the caponata. Add the almonds and let cool before serving.

PASTA ALLA NORMA

Pasta with tomato sauce and aubergines (eggplants)

Preparation time: 30 minutes + 30 minutes salting
Cooking time: 45 minutes
Serves 4

- 2 small aubergines (eggplants), sliced
- 2 tablespoons olive oil, plus extra for deep-frying
- 1 clove garlic, peeled
- 350 g/12 oz tomatoes or 500g /1 lb 2 oz (2 cups) passata (puréed canned tomatoes)
- 350 g/12 oz penne
- 100 g/3½ oz hard ricotta cheese, grated
- 8 basil leaves
- salt and pepper

Sprinkle the aubergine (eggplant) slices with salt, layering them in a colander, and let stand for 30 minutes, then rinse and pat dry with paper towels. Heat the oil for deep-frying in a deep-fryer to 180°C/350°F or until a cube of bread browns in 30 seconds. Add the aubergines and cook for 8–10 minutes until golden brown. Remove with a slotted spoon and drain on paper towels. Keep warm.

Heat the 2 tablespoons of oil in a shallow pan, add the garlic clove and cook over low heat, stirring frequently, for a few minutes until lightly browned, then remove and discard. Add the tomatoes, if using, to the pan and cook, shaking the pan occasionally, for 10 minutes, until softened and pulpy, then season to taste with salt and pepper. Alternatively, heat the passata (puréed canned tomatoes) and season to taste with salt and pepper.

Bring a large pan of salted water to a boil, add the pasta, bring back to a boil and cook for about 10 minutes, or according to package instructions, until al dente. Remove from the heat, drain, and tip onto a serving dish. Sprinkle with half the grated ricotta, spoon half the tomato sauce on top and add the basil leaves. Top with the slices of aubergine, sprinkle with the remaining ricotta and cover with the remaining tomato sauce. Serve immediately.

PARMIGIANA DI MELANZANE

Aubergine (Eggplant) Parmigiana

Preparation time: 1 hour 45 minutes + 1 hour soaking
Cooking time: 30 minutes
Serves 6–8

- — 2.5 kg/5½ lb aubergines (eggplants), sliced
- — 2 tablespoons coarse salt
- — 600 ml/1 pint (2½ cups) olive oil
- — 1.6 kg/3½ lb tomatoes, peel, seeded and chopped, or 1 kg/2¼ lb canned chopped tomatoes
- — pinch of sugar (optional)
- — 150 g/5 oz (1⅔ cups) grated Parmesan cheese
- — ½ bunch of basil, shredded
- — 3 hard-boiled eggs, sliced
- — 3 eggs
- — salt and pepper

Put the aubergine (eggplant) slices into a bowl, pour in water to cover and add the coarse salt. Put a weight on top to keep the slices submerged and let soak for 1 hour. Drain and pat dry with paper towels. Heat the oil in a frying pan or skillet, add the aubergine slices, in batches, and cook for about 10 minutes, until lightly browned on both sides. Remove with a slotted spoon and drain on paper towels.

Put the tomatoes into a shallow pan and cook over high heat, stirring frequently, for about 15 minutes, until thickened. Season with salt to taste and add a little sugar if the sauce is too acid.

Preheat the oven to 180°C/350°F/Gas Mark 4.

Put one-third of the aubergine slices on the bottom of an ovenproof dish, sprinkle with 2–3 tablespoons Parmesan, a pinch of pepper and half the shredded basil. Put half the hard-boiled eggs on top and cover with half the tomato sauce. Make another layer with half the remaining aubergine slices, 2–3 tablespoons Parmesan, a pinch of pepper, the remaining basil, the rest of the hard-boiled eggs and the remaining sauce. Top with the remaining aubergine slices. Beat the eggs with the remaining Parmesan and pour the mixture over the aubergines. Bake for about 30 minutes, until golden and bubbling, then remove from the oven and serve warm.

PISTACHIOS

Young pistachios grow on a tree in Bronte. As the pistachio matures it turns from green to pink and eventually splits to reveal the seed inside.

The best pistachios come from Bronte, a village on the western side of Mount Etna. Called the Bronte Red or Pistacchio Verde di Bronte DOP, they are encased by a hard shell, and the interior nut is emerald green with a red husk. More of a seed than a nut, it is resonant with fat and slightly resinous in flavour. This is the only place they grow in Europe, their string roots thriving in the volcanic earth and producing hand-picked fruit every other year. They are most commonly found in desserts, but pistachios are also used in savoury dishes such as pasta, or as a coating for meat or seafood. Most gelaterie in Sicily offer pistachio gelato, and the authentic recipe can be identified by the colour, a rather drab green. Neon green mixtures have surely been enhanced by an artificial colouring. The annual pistachio *sagra*, or festival, is on the second Sunday in October. In Bronte there is also the museum of the *carretto Siciliano*, the lovely hand-painted Sicilian carts of the past.

Following pages:
Pistachio is a classic Sicilian flavour and can be found for sale at markets throughout the island. The nuts are sold both whole and shelled.

GELATO

The traditional Sicilian breakfast of ice cream-stuffed brioche makes for a decadent start to the day

The Sicilian breakfast is one of the best in the world. A fresh brioche stuffed with gelato and a shot of espresso: it doesn't get much better than that! Gelato has as many regional variations as pasta, and the frozen specialities you find in Sicily are very different from what you would find in Piemonte at the food of the Alps. This is a result of the varied climate, and also of the availability of different ingredients, especially dairy. In a hot climate, such as Sicily, a rich, custard-based frozen dessert will only cool you for a few minutes; soon the digestion of all the cream and eggs you have just ingested will heat your body up. Better the fruit-based sorbets and granita that can be found in every town. Many artisanal producers use milk, but rather than thicken it with fat-rich ingredients, they use carob flour, which thrives in southern Sicily.

GELATO AL PISTACCHIO

Pistachio ice cream

Preparation time: 25 minutes + 20 minutes freezing
Cooking time: 15 minutes
Serves 6

- 750 ml/1¼ pints (3 cups) milk
- 2 tablespoons vanilla sugar
- 100 g/3½ oz (scant 1 cup) unsalted shelled pistachios, finely chopped
- 6 egg yolks
- 175 g/6 oz (scant 1 cup) caster (superfine) sugar

Bring the milk to a boil, stir in the vanilla sugar and remove the pan from the heat. Put the pistachios into a bowl and stir in a few tablespoonfuls of the milk until combined, then stir in the remaining milk. Beat the egg yolks with the sugar in another bowl until frothy, then add pistachio mixture and pour into a pan. Bring the mixture just to a boil over moderate heat, stirring constantly, then immediately remove the pan from the heat.

Let cool, then pour the mixture into an ice cream maker and freeze for about 20 minutes or according to the manufacturer's instructions.

VIII

RAGUSA

Previous page:
The ancient town of Ragusa is situated on the side of a limestone hill, sheltered between two deep valleys.

Once considered off the beaten path for tourists, the province of Ragusa has now become a true foodie destination. Home to exquisite ingredients, many young chefs that left to try their hand in other parts of the world have now returned to their roots and are attracting international attention.

The city of Ragusa is really two towns that were joined in 1926. Now called Upper Ragusa and Ragusa Ibla, the area, along with Modica and Noto (just across the border in Siracusa province), was badly damaged by a violent earthquake in 1693. When rebuilt in the eighteenth century, these towns came to be known for their romantic, honey-coloured Baroque architecture. The heart of Ragusa province lies in Ragusa Ibla and Modica, which have many similarities and a friendly rivalry that dates back many generations. In each town there is a stunning cathedral dedicated to San Giorgio, but it is Ragusa that claims him as a patron saint. Like Ragusa, Modica is divided into upper and lower cities connected by countless stairs winding in and out of the lovely palazzi and churches.

Between Siracusa and Ragusa, the land is punctuated by the valleys and dales of the Monti Iblei (Hyblean Mountains). In one gorge, Cava Ispica, there are prehistoric tombs dating back 3,000 years, and a watermill that has been restored by the original family as a charming private museum of country life. Thanks to the lush vegetation and wild mountainous areas, a fragrant honey from this area has earned great appreciation.

As if the mild growing season weren't long enough, the coast is lined with hothouses that produce some of the earliest spring vegetables, and later provide some protection from the summer's hot sun. The land is fertile and provides much of Sicily's produce and many exports to the mainland. Almonds, olives and grapes grow well here. Vittoria is a particularly good grape-growing area, and one of the island's most popular wines, the full-bodied red Cerasuola della Vittoria DOCG, is found here.

The giant white onions of the province, Giarratana, are renowned for being sweet and aromatic. Carob is another important product of the region; the pungent beans are milled to make food gum (a thickener), liqueur and flour to use in pastries. Another excellent use of the carob tree's widespread branches is as shade for the cattle, as well as fodder.

This area has one of the highest populations of cattle in Sicily. The unpasteurized whole milk is transformed into the ancient, rustic, golden-coloured Ragusano DOP cheese, which is shaped in hot water (by a method called *pasta filata*, or 'spun paste') and moulded into a large block with rounded edges that weighs up to 16 kilograms (35 pounds). Sometimes you can see the shallow, grooved impressions made by the cords used to hang it while it ages. The definition of the production area includes mountains and foothills in Ragusa and Siracusa provinces. Once it is brined, the cheese is aged for six months, and rubbed occasionally with a mixture of oil and vinegar. Another cheese, *caciocavallo ibleo*, is also made from cows' milk, along with the *tumazzo modicano* (made with milk from the Modica breed of cow), all produced using traditional methods. While pork is the most commonly consumed meat, thanks to the popularity of the area's cheeses, cows are also on the menu with beef dishes, such as tripe (flavoured with almonds, cinnamon and peppers), *'mpanatigghi* (half-moon shaped pastries, described below), and *polpettine in agrodolce*, sweet and sour meatballs (page 240).

Many other wonderful dishes are found in this area. *Tinniruma* soup (page 236) is a popular dish with peasant roots that has now been elevated to high cuisine in some restaurants. *Tinniruma* are the large

Tinniruma, the green leaves and delicate tendrils of the cucuzza squash, is one of the unique ingredients that is synonymous with the cuisine of Ragusa.

green leaves of cucuzza, a long thin green serpent-like squash. *Frittedda* (page 239) is found all over the island, especially in the spring. It is a glorious mixture of broad (fava) beans, peas and artichokes liberally seasoned with spring onions (scallions), mint and a bit of vinegar and sugar.

Sweets rise to a new level here. Modica chocolate is a world unto itself (page 245), and it has contributed to the lovely assortment of pastries you will find there. Other local classics include *mustazzola* (a filled biscuit or cookie, rich with honey and almonds), and soft *tarallucci*. While the half-moon shaped panzerotti are usually savoury, much like a calzone, here ricotta panzerotti (page 246) are short pastries filled with sweetened ricotta.

Following pages:
Ragusa is known for its large number of cattle and the production of dairy products.

HONEY

With the abundant vegetation comes flowers, and with flowers come bees and their glorious honey. Honeys vary greatly, taking their characteristics from the type of bloom in the area where the bees have their hive. They can also vary according to the season, depending on what is in bloom. For example, the almond and orange blossoms in the spring give a very different honey from what is gathered in the summer, when thyme, eucalyptus, thistle and clover are blooming. Even in December, when the carob trees bloom, a special flavour can be detected. Honey from Ragusa province is well known, especially the wild thyme honey, exquisite with the local pecorino or Ragusano cheese: a match made in heaven. Chiaramonte Gulfi, a small fourteenth-century town on the edge of the thyme-covered Monti Iblei, produces a historic fragrant honey that was praised by Virgil, Ovid and Pliny the Elder. Harvested in late June, the colour of thyme honey is amber, and it has an intense and pungent flavour.

Sicily's varied plant life means that the island produces many varieties of honey. Honey from Ragusa is well known for its distinctive aroma of thyme.

MINESTRA DI TINNIRUMA

Tinniruma soup

Tinniruma, also known as tenerume, are the tips, leaves and tendrils of the Sicilian squash Lagenaria siceraria. It is sometimes available from farmers' markets and Italian delicatessens. If you can't find it, you could use the leaves and tendrils of courgettes (zucchini) or even pea shoots.

Preparation time: 30 minutes
Cooking time: 20 minutes
Serves 4

- 2 kg/4½ lb tinniruma
- 200 g/7 oz spaghetti
- olive oil, for drizzling
- salt

Cut the squash tendrils into short lengths. Bring 500 ml/18 fl oz (generous 2 cups) lightly salted water to a boil in a pan. Add the tinniruma and cook for 10 minutes. Break up the spaghetti, add it to the pan, bring back to a boil and cook for about 10 minutes, or according to package directions, until the pasta is al dente. Ladle the soup into a tureen, drizzle with 2 rings of oil and serve immediately.

FRITTEDDA

Vegetable stew

Preparation time: 20 minutes
Cooking time: 40 minutes
Serves 8

- 4 tablespoons lemon juice, strained
- 8 globe artichokes
- 100 ml/3½ fl oz (scant ½ cup) olive oil
- 1 large onion, thinly sliced
- 1.5 kg/3¼lb (10 cups) shelled broad (fava) beans
- 1.5 kg/3¼ lb (10 cups) shelled peas
- 1 tablespoon sugar or to taste
- 3 tablespoons white wine vinegar
- salt and pepper

Half-fill a bowl with water and stir in the lemon juice. Break off the artichoke stems, remove and discard any tough outer leaves and any chokes. Cut them into wedges and plunge into the bowl of acidulated water with added lemon juice.

Heat 2 tablespoons of the oil in a pan, add the onion and cook over low heat, stirring occasionally, for 5 minutes, until softened and translucent. Drain the artichoke wedges well, add to the pan and cook for a few minutes, then add the beans. Pour in hot water to cover and simmer for 10 minutes. Add the peas and simmer for another 20 minutes, until the vegetables are tender. Season to taste with salt and pepper.

Stir the sugar into the vinegar, drizzle it over the vegetables, increase the heat to high and cook for 5 minutes, until it has evaporated. Transfer the stew to a serving dish and let cool completely before serving.

POLPETTINE IN AGRO-DOLCE

Sweet-and-sour meatballs

Preparation time: 20 minutes
Cooking time: 1 hour
Serves 6–8

- 500 g/1 lb 2 oz lean veal, minced (ground) twice
- 150–200 g/5–7 oz (2–3 cups) grated pecorino cheese
- 150 g/5 oz (3 cups) fresh breadcrumbs
- 1 clove garlic, finely chopped
- 1 tablespoon chopped flat-leaf parsley
- 2–3 eggs, lightly beaten
- vegetable oil, for deep-frying
- salt

For the sauce

- 1 onion, chopped
- 150 g/5 oz (1 cup) giardiniera
- 80 g/3 oz (⅓ cup) sugar
- 100 ml/3½ fl oz (scant ½ cup) red wine vinegar
- 800 g/1¾ lb (3 cups) tomato sauce

Mix together the veal, pecorino, breadcrumbs, garlic, parsley, eggs and a pinch of salt in a bowl, adding a little water if necessary to make a firm, even mixture. Take a small amount of the mixture at a time and shape into a ball between the palms of your hands, then gently flatten. Pour oil into a frying pan or skillet to a depth of about 10 cm/4 inches and heat. Add the meatballs, in batches if necessary, and cook, turning once, for 10–15 minutes until golden brown on both sides. Remove with a fish slice (spatula) and drain on paper towels.

To make the sauce, transfer 4–5 tablespoons of the oil used to cook the meatballs to a pan and heat. Add the onion and cook over medium-low heat, stirring occasionally, for 8–10 minutes, until golden brown. Add the giardiniera and cook for a few minutes more. Mix the sugar with 100 ml/3½ fl oz (scant ½ cup) hot water and stir into the pan with the vinegar and tomato sauce. Taste and add more sugar or more vinegar if necessary.

Simmer for a few minutes, then add the meatballs and cook for another 10 minutes. Transfer to a serving dish and serve at room temperature.

PASTA CON BROCCOLI E ALICI

Pasta with broccoli and anchovies

Preparation time: 20 minutes
Cooking time: 35 minutes
Serves 4

- 1 kg/2¼ lb broccoli, broken into florets
- 80g/3 oz salted anchovies
- 3 tablespoons olive oil
- 2 cloves garlic, peeled
- ½ chilli
- 350 g/12 oz cavatelli or pasta shells
- salt

Bring a pan of salted water to a boil, add the broccoli and cook for 5 minutes, until tender.

Meanwhile, open out the anchovies and place on a board, cut side down. Press along the backbones with your thumb, then turn the fish over and remove the backbones, snipping them at the tail end with scissors. Rinse under cold running water to remove some of the salt, then pat dry with paper towels.

Drain the broccoli. Heat the olive oil in a frying pan or skillet, add the garlic cloves and chilli and cook over low heat, stirring occasionally, for 2–3 minutes. Add the anchovies and cook, mashing the fish with a fork, until they have almost completely disintegrated. Remove and discard the garlic and chilli, then stir in the broccoli. Reduce the heat to very low and cook for 15 minutes.

Meanwhile, bring a large pan of salted water to a boil, add the pasta, bring back to a boil and cook for about 10 minutes, or according to package instructions, until al dente. Drain and tip into the pan with the sauce, increase the heat to high and toss for a few minutes. Serve immediately.

CHOCOLATE

Modica is famous for its chocolate and chocolate-based confectionaries. Different from the tempered and emulsified chocolates found in most parts of the world today, Modica's cold-processed version mirrors the granular Aztec style that can be traced back to American traditions brought to Sicily by the Spaniards in the 1500s. It starts with cocoa beans that are toasted and ground, then cooked at a low temperature at which the sugar does not melt, allowing the original flavours to maintain their integrity. The original technique was to grind the chocolate by hand with vanilla or cinnamon. Today's versions have other aromatic infusions, such as ginger, peperoncino, orange, coffee and more. Pistachio, almonds and dried fruits are also sometimes added.

A unique ingredient such as this has led to unique preparations. One favourite is rabbit roasted with unsweetened chocolate sauce. Chocolate is sometimes also found grated over caponata to make baroque caponata. Chocolate can be found mixed with peperoncino in a savoury meat sauce, and perhaps the most popular recipe is the *'mpanatigghi*, pastry pockets stuffed with aubergine (eggplant) or meat, almonds and eggs, seasoned with chocolate and spices such as cinnamon and cloves.

Chocolate was introduced to Sicily from South America whilst under Spanish rule and the distinctive granular chocolate still made in Modica is based on traditional Aztec methods of production.

PANZEROTTI DI RICOTTA

Sweet ricotta pastries

Preparation time: 50 minutes
Cooking time: 1 hour
Serves 6

- 500 g/1 lb 2 oz (4 cups) plain (all-purpose) flour, plus extra for dusting
- 100 g/3½ oz (½ cup) caster (superfine) sugar
- 100 g/3½ oz (7 tablespoons) butter or 100 g/3½ oz (½ cup) lard
- vegetable oil, for deep-frying
- icing (confectioners') sugar, for dusting
- unsweetened cocoa powder, for dusting

For the filling

- 1 kg/2¼ lb (4 cups) sheep's milk ricotta cheese
- 250 g/9 oz (1¼ cups) caster (superfine) sugar
- 200 g/7 oz dark (semisweet) chocolate, chopped

First, make the dough. Sift the flour into a mound on a counter and make a well in the centre. Add the sugar, butter or lard and enough water to mix to a smooth, elastic dough. Divide the dough into 2–3 pieces and roll out each piece into a thin sheet on a lightly floured surface.

To make the filling, rub the ricotta through a sieve (strainer) into a bowl. Add the sugar and beat well until thoroughly incorporated and the mixture is creamy. Stir in the chocolate.

Put small mounds of the filling evenly spaced on one side of a sheet of dough, then fold over the uncovered side and press around the filling with your fingers. Cut out the panzerotti into squares or crescents with a cookie cutter. Repeat with the remaining sheets of dough and filling until they are all used.

Pour the oil into a large frying pan or skillet to a depth of about 10 cm/4 inches and heat. Add the panzerotti, in batches if necessary, and cook for 8–10 minutes, until golden brown. Remove with a slotted spoon and drain on paper towels, then let cool. Dust with icing (confectioners') sugar and unsweetened cocoa powder before serving.

S.P.Q.N.

IX

SIRACUSA

Siracusa is one of Sicily's most ancient cities, founded by the Corinthians in 734 BC, and at that time it rivalled Athens in importance. The oldest part of the city is a picturesque island called Ortigia, the source of fresh water and of the myth of Artemis and Arethusa. Legend has it that Artemis changed Arethusa into a spring to escape the angry river god, and when she returned to her physical body, the spring remained. Nearby, the Teatro Greco, with seating for 15,000 spectators, still stands. Inside the Duomo, the remains of the ancient Doric temple of Athena from the fifth century BC are still visible. Over time, the Greek influence has remained an important patrimony for the lifestyle and cuisine of the province. Besides the many ingredients imported by the Greeks, dishes such as Aubergine (Eggplant) Parmigiano could have well been influenced by the Greek moussaka, with its layers of aubergine, tomato sauce and cheese.

Previous page:
The impressive façade of Noto Cathedral. The cathedral had to be rebuilt in 1996 following a part collapse as a result of an earthquake.

Further south, Noto has a certain reputation for sweets. The Caffé Sicilia, founded in 1892, has world-wide reputation for the gelati made with local ingredients, such as almonds, chocolate and essences, such as orange blossoms and jasmine. A sweet, very Arabic, speciality of Noto is the *giuggiulena* (also called *cubbaita*), which could best be described as crunchy sesame nougat. The nicest ones are made with sesame, thyme honey from Iblei, almonds from Avola and orange zest from Siracusa.

Bottarga from the fishing village of Marzamemi is growing in popularity. The egg sack from freshly caught tuna is pressed and salted to create a cured condiment that is grated over pasta instead of cheese, imparting a unique marine flavour. Siracusa province is renowned for citrus fruits, blood oranges and lemons in particular. The Tarocco orange, packed with 40 per cent more vitamin C than other oranges, has a vibrant orange and red pulp, yet looks like a regular orange from the outside. It first appeared near the town of

Francofonte some time in the eighteenth century, a spontaneous variation on another sweet orange. Local culinary guide Anita Iaconangelo advises that 'the colour of the skin of the Tarocco blood orange gives little clue as to what is inside. Sometimes the skin is uniformly orange, or it can be blushed with red, as though embarrassed to reveal its voluptuous flesh.' Oranges are used not only in desserts, but also in savoury dishes. There is nothing more appealing than fresh sausages on the grill, and we have already seen that wild fennel is an important ingredient in Sicilian cuisine; here, the minced (ground) pork is seasoned with fennel seeds and served with fresh orange slices.

In December, the celebratory dish *cuccìa* is served or the festival of Santa Lucia, the patron saint of Siracusa. Whole wheat is cooked in sweetened milk and laced with chocolate to celebrate the shipment of wheat that arrived during a famine on the feast day of Santa Lucia.

NERO D'AVOLA

This full-bodied red wine is one of Italy's indigenous varieties of grape, and has been part of the scene for hundreds of years. Winemaking methods have improved a great deal in recent years, and it has become one of the island's most popular wines. Sometimes blended with other grapes, the monoculture has a flavour that is fruity and peppery, much like a Syrah. It pairs nicely with lamb, game and aged cheeses.

Opposite and following pages: Sicily's sun-drenched climate and rich volcanic soil make it the perfect place to grow grapes. Nero d'Avola, the island's most widely grown variety, ripens under the summer sun and is harvested in September.

TOMATOES

Tomatoes are not indigenous to Italy. Introduced in the 1500s along with many foods from the New World, they were not recognized as a food product until the 1700s… and then they literally took root in Italian cuisine. Italians view tomatoes as either sauce tomatoes (*da salsa*) or to be eaten raw (*insalatari*). Many prefer their salad tomatoes slightly green and acidic, whereas sauce tomatoes are riper and meatier. Since genetic modification (GMO or OGM) is not allowed in Italy, the flavours are original and rich. Some tomatoes have been naturally selected for their special qualities, so new varieties specific to the unique climate and soil of an area have evolved. For example, in the region of Campania you find the San Marzano tomato, and in Sicily there is the Pachino tomato, a DOP variety that has been cultivated since the 1920s in Pachino, one of Europe's southernmost towns.

The year-round mild climate influences the distinctive Pachino, as well as the salinity of the water used to irrigate the plants. Shiny and firm, intense and sweet, there are four types of Pachino cultivars: Ciliegino (cherry), Costoluto (ribbed), Tondo Liscio (smooth and round), and Grappolo (clustered bunches). The DOP regulates the zone for growing these tomatoes, bordered on the north by Noto, on the south by Portopalo di Capo Passero, and reaching into Ragusa province as far west as Ispica.

In full summer, when the tomatoes are ripe, women all over the island start making the dark, sunbaked *'strattu* or *estratto*, which literally means 'extraction.' This is a process that extracts the essence of the tomato, and is the 'secret ingredient' found in many recipes. The flavour is different from simply cooking down tomatoes, as the freshness of the tomato is still discernible. Only a spoonful is necessary in a soup, for example, to ramp up the flavour factor. Melting a little in olive oil at the start of a dish also adds character:

As in the rest of Italy, tomatoes are a cornerstone of Sicilian cuisine.

meat sauces, octopus, sausages and pasta are all improved with this subtle addition. All you need to make this yourself is strong sun with daytime temperatures of around 38°C (100°F), and enough space to set up a few trays. The women start by cooking the tomatoes very briefly to soften them. It is important not to overcook them, or that special, fresh flavour will disappear. Once softened, they are passed through a food mill to remove the skin and seeds. This purée is salted, then spread thinly onto large platters or wooden trays and placed in the direct sun. Stirred occasionally, then spread flat again, the paste is left to concentrate for a few days. When it has become a deep, dark, thick, almost leathery red paste, it is packed into jars, covered with a layer of olive oil, and kept in a cool place to use all winter long. It is extremely concentrated; it takes a good 5 kilograms (11 pounds) of tomatoes to make 250 grams (9 ounces) of *'strattu*.

Another method of preserving tomatoes is to sun dry them. The firm tomato is cut in half, but left attached on one side, so that it opens like a book. Arranged on a large tray, they are left in full sun for the day, and brought inside house at night. Each day they are brought back out into the sun until they reach the desired consistency. These dried tomatoes add zing to many dishes, or can be prepared on their own. A favourite is *pomodori secchi ripieni*, stuffed dried tomatoes, which makes a great appetizer.

When summer is at its peak and the tomatoes are ripe, kitchens all over Sicily are put to work making a *'strattu*, a strongly flavoured tomato paste

POMODORI RIPIENI FRITTI

Fried stuffed tomatoes

Preparation time: 30 minutes + 30 minutes standing
Cooking time: 40 minutes
Serves 6

- — 12 plum tomatoes, preferably San Marzano
- — 3 tablespoons olive oil
- — salt

For the filling

- — 300 g/11 oz (6 cups) fresh white breadcrumbs
- — 50 g/2 oz (⅔ cup) grated pecorino or caciocavallo cheese
- — 1 clove garlic, finely chopped
- — 3 tablespoons chopped flat-leaf parsley
- — salt and pepper

Halve the tomatoes, scoop out the seeds with a teaspoon and sprinkle the insides with salt. Put them upside down on paper towels and let stand for 30 minutes to drain.

Make the filling. Put the breadcrumbs, cheese, garlic and parsley into a bowl, season with salt and pepper and stir in a little water to mix. Fill the tomato halves with this mixture.

Heat the oil in a frying pan or skillet, add the tomato halves and cook over low heat for 30 minutes or until browned and cooked through. Remove from the pan and serve hot or at room temperature.

PER ALIMENTI
1 litro

CAPONATA DI VERDURE

Wild vegetable caponata

There are many theories as to how the name caponata came about. One is that it comes from the fish cappone (gurnard or sea robin) which was once one of the ingredients. Fishermen added whatever fish remained unsold, and more sophisticated recipes added octopus to the caponata. The Spanish version included shellfish. As time went on, fish disappeared from the dish but the vegetables remained. Caponata is an antipasto to be enjoyed on warm bread such as bruschetta, as well as a side dish that goes especially well with fish.

Preparation time: 40 minutes
Cooking time: 40 minutes
Serves 4–6

- 2 kg/4½ lb mixed wild vegetables, such as wild chicory (curly endive), trimmed
- 2–3 tablespoons olive oil
- 1 celery stalk, chopped
- 1 onion, thinly sliced
- 2 tablespoons red wine vinegar
- salt

Cook the mixed vegetables in plenty of salted boiling water until just tender, then drain well.

Heat the oil in a frying pan or skillet, add the celery and onion and cook over low heat, stirring occasionally, for 5 minutes, until softened. Add the mixed vegetables and cook for a few minutes more. Season to taste with salt, sprinkle with the vinegar, stir and remove from the heat. Serve warm or cold.

CONIGLIO DEI NEBRODI IN AGRODOLCE

Sweet-and-sour Nebrodi rabbit

Preparation time: 30 minutes + 30 minutes soaking
Cooking time: 2 hours
Serves 4–6

- 300 ml/½ pint (1¼ cups) red wine vinegar
- 1 × 1.5-kg 3¼-lb rabbit, cut into pieces
- 3 tablespoons olive oil
- 2 onions, thinly sliced
- 1 celery stalk, chopped
- 1 tablespoon tomato purée (paste)
- 250 g/9 oz (2 cups) giardiniera, chopped
- 4–5 apples, peeled, cored, sliced and blanched in acidulated water
- 3 tablespoons sugar
- 50 g/2 oz (½ cup) shelled hazelnuts, roasted and chopped
- wild fennel, to garnish
- salt

Stir 200 ml/7 fl oz (scant 1 cup) of the vinegar into a bowl of water. Add the pieces of rabbit and let soak for 30 minutes, then drain and pat dry.

Heat the olive oil in a large non-stick frying pan or skillet, add the pieces of rabbit and cook over medium-high heat, turning occasionally, for 8–10 minutes, until evenly browned. Remove the pan from the heat.

Pour water into a small frying pan or skillet to a depth of 1.5 cm/¾ inch, add a pinch of salt and set over medium-low heat. Add the onions and celery and cook for about 15 minutes, until the onions have become translucent.

Mix the tomato purée (paste) with 200 ml/7 fl oz (scant 1 cup) hot water. Transfer the pieces of rabbit to a large pan, add the tomato purée mixture and the onion and celery mixture, cover and simmer for 45 minutes. Stir in the giardiniera and the apples, re-cover the pan and simmer for another 45 minutes.

Heat the remaining vinegar in a small pan, then remove from the heat, stir in the sugar and add to the pan of rabbit. Season to taste with salt and remove the pan from the heat.

Transfer the stew to a serving dish and let cool, then sprinkle with the hazelnuts and garnish with the wild fennel.

GELO DI CAFFÈ

Coffee jelly (gelatin)

This type of dessert is very common in Sicily and hugely popular in the summer. Other common versions include those flavoured with jasmine flowers, prickly pear or watermelon.

Preparation time: 15 minutes + 3 hours chilling
Cooking time: 30 minutes
Serves 4

- 500 ml/18 fl oz (2 cups) fairly strong freshly brewed coffee
- 1 teaspoon ground cinnamon
- 80 g/3 oz (⅓ cup) caster (superfine) sugar
- 40 g/1½ oz (⅓ cup) cornflour (cornstarch) or arrowroot

Rinse out a 500-ml/18-fl oz (2-cup) decorative mould with cold water. While the coffee is still hot, pour it into a bowl, stir in the cinnamon, then add the sugar and continue to stir until cooled slightly. Sift the cornflour (cornstarch) or arrowroot into the mixture and whisk to prevent any lumps from forming.

Strain the mixture into a pan and bring to a boil over very low heat, stirring constantly. Remove the pan from the heat, stir for a few seconds and then pour into the prepared mould.

Chill in the refrigerator for at least 3 hours. To serve, remove from the refrigerator and turn out the mould onto a serving dish.

INDEX

Page numbers in bold refer to the illustrations

E

F

G

H

I

L

M

N

O

P

R

S

T

V

W

Phaidon Press Limited
2 Cooperage Yard
London E15 2QR

Phaidon Press Inc.
111 Broadway
New York, NY 10006

Phaidon SARL
55, rue Traversière
75012 Paris

www.phaidon.com

First published 2013
Published in this format 2026

ISBN: 978 1 83729 246 2

Sicily originates from *Il cucchiaio d'argento Cucina Regionale*, first published in 2008.

A CIP catalogue record for this book is available from the British Library.

Commissioning Editor: Emma Robertson
Project Editor: Daniel Hurst
Production Controller: Vanessa Todd-Holmes

Narrative text by Pamela Sheldon Johns
Photographs by Edward Park
Illustrations by Beppe Giacobbe
Designed by Sonya Dyakova

Printed in China

The publishers would like to thank Chiara Agnello, Maria Teresa Allegra, Aldo Bacciulli, Eleonora Briguglia, Laura Briguglia, Alberto Comai, Mary Consonni, Linda Doeser, Carmen Figini, Nicole Grimsdale, Jacob Kennedy, Margot Levy, Adriana Moscuzza, Domenica Proetto, Oliver Rowe, Daniela Silva, Susan Spaull, Maria Grazia Santuccio, for their contributions to the book.

RECIPE NOTES

Butter should always be unsalted.

Pepper is always freshly ground black pepper, unless otherwise specified.

Eggs, vegetables and fruits are assumed to be medium size, unless otherwise specified. For US, use large eggs unless otherwise specified.

Milk is always whole, unless otherwise specified.

Garlic cloves are assumed to be large; use two if yours are small.

Ham means cooked ham, unless otherwise specified.

Prosciutto refers exclusively to raw, dry-cured ham, usually from Parma or San Daniele in northern Italy.

Cooking and preparation times are for guidance only, as individual ovens vary. If using a fan oven, follow the manufacturer's instructions concerning oven temperatures.

To test whether your deep-frying oil is hot enough, add a cube of stale bread. If it browns in thirty seconds, the temperature is 180–190°C (350–375°F), about right for most frying. Exercise caution when deep frying: add the food carefully to avoid splashing, wear long sleeves, and never leave the pan unattended.

Some recipes include raw or very lightly cooked eggs. These should be avoided particularly by the elderly, infants, pregnant women, convalescents, and anyone with an impaired immune system.

All herbs, shoots, flowers and leaves should be picked fresh from a clean source.

Do exercise caution when foraging for ingredients, which should only be eaten if an expert has deemed them safe to eat. In particular, do not gather wild mushrooms yourself before seeking the advice of an expert who has confirmed their suitability for human consumption.

As some species of mushrooms have been known to cause allergic reaction and illness, do take extra care when cooking and eating mushrooms and do seek immediate medical help if you experience a reaction after preparing or eating them.

All spoon measurements are level. 1 teaspoon = 5 ml; 1 tablespoon = 15 ml. Australian standard tablespoons are 20 ml, so Australian readers are advised to use 3 teaspoons in place of 1 tablespoon when measuring small quantities.

Cup, metric and imperial measurements are given throughout, and US equivalents are given in brackets. Follow one set of measurements, not a mixture, as they are not interchangeable.